D1571586

"Only with you, Hafez, do I wish to compete, for the older you get the younger you become . . . And religion is no obstacle, for if the word 'Islam' means to submit to God, we all live and die in Islam."

Johann Wolfgang Goethe

"Oh Hafez. Give me thought—
In fiery figures cast,
For all beside is naught
All else is din and blast . . ."

Ralph Waldo Emerson

H A F E Z
D A N C E   O F   L I F E

VERSE TRANSLATION
Michael Boylan

ILLUMINATION
Hossein Zenderoudi

PROSE TRANSLATION
Wilberforce Clarke

PERSIAN CALLIGRAPHY
Amir Hossein Tabnak

AFTERWORD
Michael C. Hillmann

MAGE PUBLISHERS
1988

CONTENTS

FOREWORD

When I was a child, my father taught me lines from the poems of Hafez before I could read. Then, every morning when he took me to school, we would play a game (*mosha'ereh*) in which he would recite one line of a poem and I would have to come up with another, beginning in the letter with which his line had ended. His greatest pleasure came when I could take on his friends at this game and win.

In Iran, poetry is a part of everyone's life, from the sweeper in the bazaar to the university don. And Khajeh Shamsoddin Mohammad Hafez-e Shirazi (c. 1320-1390), one of the great poets, is also the most popular. In the West, however, although several giants of literature have been influenced and inspired by his poetry, Hafez has for the most part remained unknown to the non-academic lover of poetry.

Reviewing the existing English verse translations, we could not find one that corresponded to our Iranian image of Hafez. We consulted the experts and were told the poetry of Hafez could not be translated. We decided to ask Hafez himself. In the age old tradition, we asked a question, "Should our publishing house, Mage, attempt a contemporary book of Hafez's poetry—both for the English speaking public and for all the young Iranians now dispersed throughout the world seeking the strengths of their heritage?" Then we opened at random Hafez's *Divan* (collected poems). The following is a stanza from the poem which appeared (*Paean of a Dreg-Drinker*, page 28):

If the young wine-selling mage	گر چنین جلوه کند مغبچهٔ باده فروش
Should thus choose to come,	
I will make my eyelash a broom	خاکروب در میخانه کنم مژگان را
And sweep the walkway clean.	

Encouraged by Hafez's offer of assistance, it was with memories of my father and my early childhood—and the fact that our sons had learned the lyrics of "chicken soup with rice" but no Hafez—that my wife and I began this project. Our goal is to make Hafez's poetry as enjoyable to readers in English as it is to Iranians and as accessible to the lay lover of poetry as it is to the linguist and scholar.

In fact, Hafez did show us the way by inspiring us to attempt in this book that which he achieves in his poetry—dipolarity and multiple points of view.

Purposely, therefore, with feet on the ground and head in the heavens (while trying not to lose balance), we have selected a very small number (12 from about 500) of Hafez's finest poems. But then for each poem we have included a multiple perspective for the reader at every level: from the lyric to the metaphysical, from free illumination to disciplined calligraphy, from contemporary verse translation to an English transliteration, and from colorful anecdote to an intellectual essay.

In this way we hope that many will be encouraged and inspired to use this book as a key to the further delights of the immortal Hafez.

Mohammad and Najmieh Batmanglij
Vence, France
4 July, 1987

HAFEZ

حافظ

Song of Spring

The gentle breeze will blow a new
Vitality to the barren earth.
The old will become young.

Persian Lilacs will offer the white lily
Their fragrant red cup.
The narcissus eye will glimpse the anemone.

Because of the tyranny of separation endured
The nightingale shall speed
Into the rose garden bursting with song.

If I've left the mosque for the tavern,
Don't complain: the ceremonies stretch on f a r   t o o   l o n g .
And time is short.

Heart, if you deposit today's joy for tomorrow
You may be left with nothing.
For who will guarantee it?

In the month before the fast
Drink your fill of wine
For this sun, too, will set
In Ramazan
These will be out of   sight.

The rose's beauty is very dear.
Enjoy its petals when it is here.
As soon as it comes it is gone.

Ministrel, for this Feast of Love sing your melody!
No more chatter of the past
Nor of the future, now.

Hafez has made the journey to Life
For you.
Bid him fond adieu for soon in death his passing he—*shall be*.

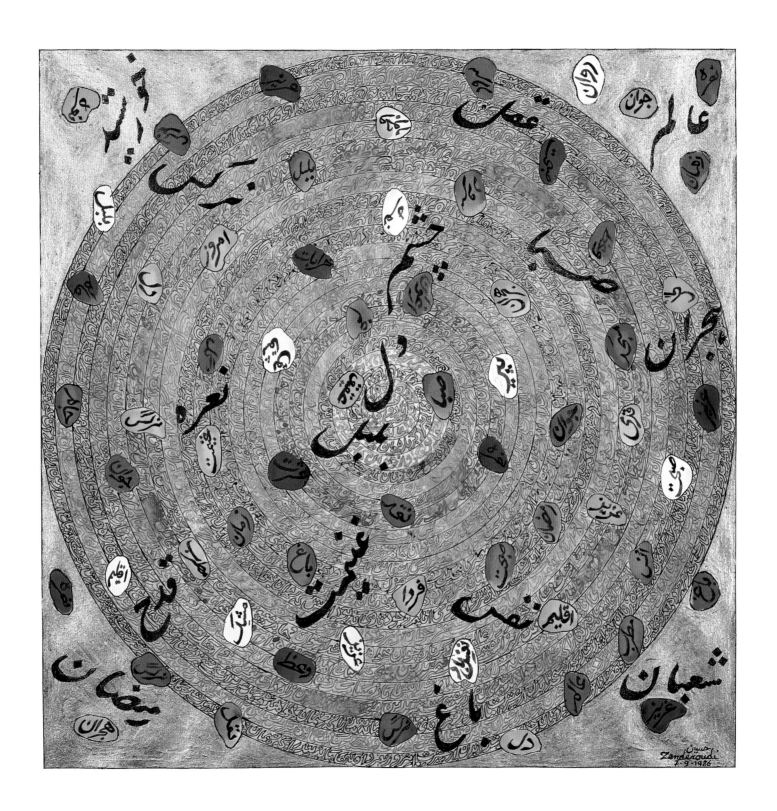

Musk-diffusing, the breath of the morning breeze—shall be:
Again the world old [by autumn and winter] young—shall be.

To the [white] lily, the [ruddy] arghavan shall give the [red] cornelian cup:
Glancing at the anemones, the eye of the narcissus—shall be.

This tyranny that, from the grief of separation, the bolbol endured
In the rose's pavilion, clamour-making—shall be.

If from the Masjed to the tavern I go, carp not:
Long is the assembly of admonition; and [short] the time [of life] shall be.

O heart! if to-morrow thou cast [postpone] the joy of to-day,
Surety for the capital of cash of permanency [till to-morrow], who—shall be?

In the month Sha'ban, put not the goblet from thy hand. For this sun,
[Only] till the night of the 'id of Ramazan out of sight—shall be.

Precious is the rose; its society reckon plunder.
For in this way to the garden it came; and, [quickly] in that way—shall go.

O Minstrel! the assembly of associate friends, it is: sing the ghazal and the ode:
How long sayest thou:—"[This moment] passed like this; and like that—shall be."

[From non-existence] to the clime of existence, came Hafez for thy sake:
Plant thy foot for farewell to him, for [quickly in death] passing he—shall be.

نَفَسِ بادِ صبا مُشکْ فشان خواهد شد 	 عالمِ پیر دگر باره جوان خواهد شد

ارغوان جامِ عقیقی به سمن خواهد داد 	 چشمِ نرگس به شقایق نگران خواهد شد

این تطاول که کشید از غمِ هجرانِ بلبل 	 تا سراپردهٔ گل نعره زنان خواهد شد

گر ز مسجد به خرابات شدم خرده مگیر 	 مجلسِ وعظ دراز است و زمان خواهد شد

ای دل ار عشرتِ امروز به فردا فکنی 	 مایهٔ نقدِ بقا را که ضمان خواهد شد

ماهِ شعبان منه از دست قدح کاین خورشید 	 از نظر تا شبِ عید رمضان خواهد شد

گل عزیز است غنیمت شمریدش صحبت 	 که به باغ آمد از این راه و از آن خواهد شد

مطربا مجلسِ انس است غزل خوان و سرود 	 چند گویی که چنین رفت و چنان خواهد شد

حافظ از بهرِ تو آمد سوی اقلیمِ وجود 	 قدمی نه به وداعش که روان خواهد شد

Morning Light

You are dawn; I am a candle
        Glowing in solitude to you.
Smile, and lo my vital spirit's yours.

Such is the pain from love's wound,
        Oh taming locks of Beauty,
That about my tomb a bed of violets will grow.

Waiting upon the threshold of your desire
        I open my eyes
That you might show me favor, but instead you retire.

Sorrow's legions, I'm ever thankful for your friendship;
        May God protect you.
When I'm forsaken, you, alone, will abide with me.

Pupil of my eye, despite your black heart,
        I am your slave
Because my heart's sorrow calls for a shower of a thousand tears.

The rising sun spreads its rays across the sky
        Revealing my love's splendor
That none observe as I.

If my love, like the whispering breeze,
        Should pass Hafez's tomb,
Then this passion shall rend my shroud in two.

Like the morning [of laughing forehead] Thou art; and the candle of the
chamber of the morning, I am:
Smile; and behold how [for Thee] my soul, I surrender.

In my heart, the stain of love for Thy heart-alluring tress is so [in dwelling] that,
When [from this vanishing world] I pass, my tomb becometh the [dark] violet-bed.

On the threshold of hope of Thee, I have opened my eye,
That Thou mayest cast one glance; from Thy glance, me Thou Thyself castedest.

O crowd of griefs! to thee, how may I utter thanks? God forgive thee!
On the day of friendlessness, at last, from my bosom thou goest not.

I am the slave of the pupil of my eye, who, notwithstanding his black-heartedness,
Raineth a thousand drops [tears], when my heart's pain, I recount.

On every side, our idol displayeth splendour; but,
This glance that I keep glancing, none seeth.

If the Beloved like the [fragrant] breeze pass to the tomb of Hafez
From desire, in the heart of that narrow place [the grave], the shroud, I rend.

تو همچو صبحی و من شمع خلوتِ سحرم   تبسمی کن و جان بین که چون همی سپرم

چنین که در دلِ من داغِ زلفِ سرکشِ تست   بنفشه زار شود تربتم چو در گذرم

بر آستانِ مرادت گشاده‌ام در چشم   که یک نظر فکنی خود فکند از نظرم

چه شکر گویمت ای خیلِ غم عفاک الله   که روزِ بیکسی آخر نمی‌روی ز سرم

غلام مردمِ چشمم که با سیاه دلی   هزار قطره ببارد چو دردِ دل شمرم

به هر نظر بتِ ما جلوه می‌کند لیکن   کس این کرشمه نبیند که من همی نگرم

بخاکِ حافظ اگر یار بگذرد چون باد   ز شوق در دلِ آن تنگنا کفن بدرم

Thorns and Roses

Forsaken Joseph
To Canaan will return.
Despair not.
Upon the thorny stalks of family grief
A rose shall bloom.
Despair not.

Turbulent, grieving heart, be sanguine.
Your temperament shall balance.
Confused head, you shall see
A new emergent unity.
Despair not.

Sweet bird, as long as there is spring,
Once more upon the meadow's throne you shall sing!
Winter shall pass and you shall find your tune.
The roses shall nod and cense you with their bloom.
Despair not.

If this spinning world in a day or two
Does not bring fortune's gifts to you
Remember, life has many turns,
No two of which bring the same return.
Despair not.

Hey! Raise those eyes for you don't see
The universe's mysteries,
Those secrets hidden from our view;
Behind the screen are games anew.
Despair not.

Though the deluge shall arrive,
And threaten everything alive,
Noah's there to be your guide,
And steer you through the typhoon's eye.
Despair not.

If desire for the Way is in your heart,
Then set yourself to depart
And plant your foot upon the sand,
Though the thorn may leave its jagged brand.
Despair not.

Though our lives may be unsafe
With purposes which we can't relate,
Remember, that in any race
There always is an end.
Despair not.

We are all *lovers*, *separated*;
Under a watchful, tenacious Eye.
For God Knows All:
Our state is His design.
Despair not.

Alone in the darkest night
Reduced to wretched poverty, Hafez.
Because you practice fervent prayer
And study the Holy Book
                              Despair not.

Back to Kan'an, lost Yusuf cometh:—suffer not grief:
One day, the sorrowful cell becometh the rose-garden:—suffer not grief.

O grief-stricken heart! better, becometh thy state; display not the ill-heart:
Back to reason, cometh this distraught head:—suffer not grief.

If on the sward's throne, again be the spring of life,
O bird, night-singing! over thy head, thou mayst draw the canopy of the
rose:—suffer not grief.

If, for a space of two days, to our desire, the sphere's revolutions turned not,
Ever, in one way, the state of revolution is not:—suffer not grief.

Ho! since thou are not acquainted with the hidden mystery, be not helpless:
Within the screen, are hidden pastimes;—suffer not grief.

Oh heart! if the foundation of·thy existence, the torrent of passing away
[mortality] pluck up,
Since Nuh is thy boat-master, of the deluge,—suffer not grief.

If, from desire [of pilgrimage] to the Ka'be thou wilt plant thy foot in the desert,
[then] if the [mighty] Arabian thorn make reproofs,—suffer not grief.

Although the stage [of this world] is very fearsome; and the purpose hidden,
There is not a road, whereof is no end;—suffer not grief.

In separation from the Beloved, and vexing [on the part] of the watcher,—our
state [of perturbation and confusion]:
All, God, our state causing, knoweth;—suffer not grief.

In the corner of poverty and in the solitude of dark nights, Hafez,
So long as thine are the practice of praying and reading of the Koran—suffer not grief.

یوسف گم‌گشته بازآید به کنعان غم مخور 	 کلبه‌ٔ احزان شود روزی گلستان غم مخور

ای دل غمدیده حالت به شود دل بد مکن 	 وین سر شوریده بازآید به سامان غم مخور

گر بهار عمر باشد باز بر تخت چمن 	 چتر گل در سر کشی ای مرغ خوشخوان غم مخور

دور گردون گر دو روزی بر مراد ما نرفت 	 دائماً یکسان نباشد حال دوران غم مخور

هان مشو نومید چون واقف نه‌ای از سرّ غیب 	 باشد اندر پرده بازیهای پنهان غم مخور

ای دل ار سیل فنا بنیاد هستی برکَنَد 	 چون تو را نوح است کشتیبان ز طوفان غم مخور

در بیابان گر به شوق کعبه خواهی زد قدم 	 سرزنشها گر کند خار مغیلان غم مخور

گرچه منزل بس خطرناک است و مقصد بس بعید 	 هیچ راهی نیست کان را نیست پایان غم مخور

حال ما در فرقت جانان و ابرام رقیب 	 جمله می‌داند خدای حال گردان غم مخور

حافظا در کنج فقر و خلوت شبهای تار 	 تا بود وردت دعا و درس قرآن غم مخور

Dance of Life

Waiting. Straining to hear—your voice
              that I may rise.
I am heaven's dove that from the earthly cage will rise.

If I am bid but to be your slave
             I gladly shall foreswear
Dominion over worldly things as now I rise.

Let the rain fall from your cloud of grace,
            oh Lord;
Before, to dust I would be changed—I rise.

Bring a minstrel to my grave and a bottle of good wine.
               Your fragrant presence
Shall lift me dancing full of joy as I rise.

Hold high your lordly stature that I may see.
           You draw me nigh.
With clapping hands I leave this life, and I rise.

Though I am old yet in a night—
          from your embrace
In Dawn's new light a youth will rise.

On the day that I die, a glimpse of you may I behold
             and, as Hafez
From Life's desire leap into eternity, and I will   r i s e !

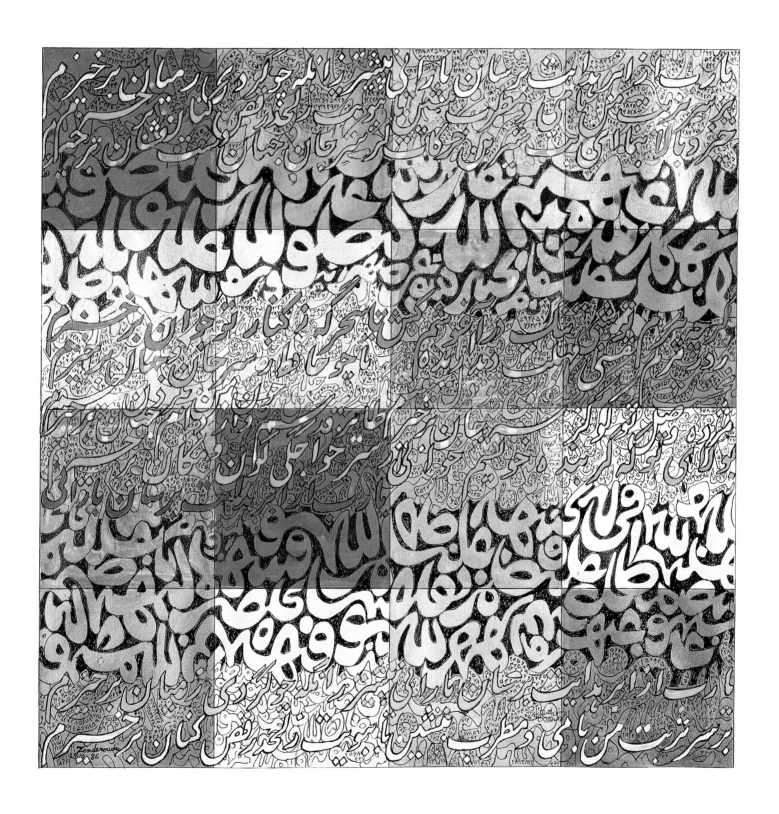

Where, the glad tidings of union with Thee, so that, from desire of life,
—I may rise?
The holy bird [of paradise] am I; from the world's snare,—I rise

By Thy love [I swear] that, if me, Thy slave, Thou call,
Out from desire of lordship of existence and dwelling [both worlds],—I rise.

O Lord! from the cloud of guidance, the rain cause to arrive:
Before that, from the midst, like a [handful of] dust,—I rise.

At the head of my tomb, with wine and the minstrel, sit:
So that by thy perfume, dancing,—I may rise.

O Idol, sweet of motion! arise; and Thy [lofty, cypress-like] stature display:
That, from desire of life and of the world, clapping —I may rise.

Though I am old, one night me, close in Thy embrace take,
So that, in the morning, from Thy embrace, young—I may rise.

On the day of my death, a breath's chance visit give me,
So that like Hafez from the desire of Life and the world—I may rise.

مژده وصل تو کو کز سرِ جان برخیزم $\qquad$ طایرِ قُدسم و از دامِ جهان برخیزم

بِوَلای تو که گر بنده خویشم خوانی $\qquad$ از سرِ خواجگی کَون و مکان برخیزم

یارب از ابرِ هدایت برسان بارانی $\qquad$ پیشتر زانکه چو گردی ز میان برخیزم

بر سرِ تُربت من با می و مُطرب بنشین $\qquad$ تا به بویت ز لَحَد رقص کنان برخیزم

خیز و بالا بنما ای بُتِ شیرین حرکت $\qquad$ کز سرِ جان و جهان دست فشان برخیزم

گرچه پیرم تو شبی تنگ در آغوشم کش $\qquad$ تا سحرگه ز کنارِ تو جوان برخیزم

روزِ مرگم نفَسی مُهلتِ دیدار بده $\qquad$ تا چو حافظ ز سرِ جان و جهان برخیزم

Paean of a Dreg-drinker

The splendor of youth, again
Has come to the garden.
The fragrance of the rose carries
A sweet message to the nightingale.

Soft breeze,
If you reach the meadow where
The cypress, rose, and sweet basil lie—
Give them my greetings.

If the young wine selling mage
Should thus choose to come,
I will make my eyelash a broom
And sweep the walkway clean.

Oh moon, do not eclipse your white beauty
With your dark flowing hair.
For then my tortured mind
Shall be a frenzy of perplexity.

Though the sophisticated scoff
At those who drink the dregs
They will lose their faith
When they arrive at the tavern door.

Stand near the blessed few.
In Noah's ark a little dust
Inherited everything.
While a drop of water was repaid
With total devastation.

Go forth from the world and seek not bread
For within the dark cup is a deadly potion.
To all whose future is to be dust
What use is it to build a tower to the sky?

My Moon of Canaan,
                                    the Throne of Egypt,
Is yours. The hour is near.
It is time to bid the prison farewell.

So drink in joy, Hafez!
And balance on the brink.
But do not twist as others have
The sacred word of God
Into a hypocritical snare of lies.

The splendour of youth's time again belongeth to the garden;
The glad tidings of the rose reacheth the bolbol sweet of song.

O breeze! if again thou reach the youths of the meadow,
Convey our service to the cypress, the rose, and the sweet basil.

If the young magian, wine-seller, display such splendour,
I will make my eye-lash the dust-sweeper of the door of the wine-house.

O thou that drawest, over the moon [of thy face], the chaugan of purest
ambergris [the black tress],—
Make not distraught of state, me of revolving head.

This crowd that laugheth at those drinking the wine-dregs, I fear?
They will, in the end, ruin their Faith.

Be the friend of the men of God; for, in Nuh's ark,
Was a little dust [humbleness], that purchased not the deluge
[the empire of the world] for a drop of water.

Forth from the house of the sphere, go; and bread, seek not.
For, in the end, this dark cup [of avarice] slayeth the guest.

To him, whose last sleeping-place is with two handfuls of earth [the grave],
Say:—"Thine what need, to exalt the turrets to the sky?"

My moon of Kan'an [my soul]! the throne of Egypt [the rank of perfection;
the world of souls] is thine:
The time is that [time] when thou shouldst bid farewell to the prison
[of the body, or of the world].

Hafez! drink wine [of love]; practise profligacy [the concealing of secrets]
and be happy [grieve not, and grieved be not]; but,
Like others, make not the Koran the snare of deceit.

رونق عهدِ شباب است دگر بستان را می‌رسد مژده گل بلبل خوش‌الحان را

ای صبا گر به جوانان چمن بازرسی خدمت ما برسان سرو و گل و ریحان را

گر چنین جلوه کند مغبچه باده‌فروش خاکروب درِ میخانه کنم مژگان را

ای که بر مَه‌کشی از عنبرِ سارا چوگان مضطرب حال مگردان منِ سرگردان را

ترسم این قوم که بر دُردکشان می‌خندند در سرِ کارِ خرابات کنند ایمان را

یارِ مردانِ خدا باش که در کشتیِ نوح هست خاکی که به آبی نخرد طوفان را

برو از خانهٔ گردون بدر و نان مطلب کان سیه‌کاسه در آخر بکشد مهمان را

هر که را خوابگه آخر مشتی خاک است گو چه حاجت که به افلاک کشی ایوان را

ماهِ کنعانیِ من مَسندِ مصر آن تو شد وقتِ آن است که بدرود کنی زندان را

حافظا می خور و رندی کن و خوش باش ولی دام تزویر مکن چون دگران قرآن را

Boatpeople

Forsake me not, oh Lord;
                    Saints in heaven have pity.
My heart falls from the grasp,
                    Oh Lord!
I am distressed that Love's sacred mystery
Should be unveiled for all to see.

We are boatpeople;
Let the gentle winds return
That we may steer toward the shore
And gaze upon our Friend once more.

The fleeting moment of blessed life
Is a many turning tale of the fantastic.
My friend, regard as precious treasure
Your comrades' love that shall endure.

Last night at the feast of the roses and wine
The nightingale sweetly sang,
"Steward, bring more wine!
The laggards must awaken."
For you are liberal in your gifts
And so we drink your health.
May one day you inquire, too
Of the poor who taste no food.

The cosmic unity may be explained
By these affinities:
        To friends give warmth
        To enemies, fair courtesy.
If You do not approve
        Of what our lives've become,
Change Our Fate.
For to the bridge of reputation
We were given no admission.

"The daughter of the grape,"
The Sufi said, "was the mother of sin"—
To us mortals, seems even sweeter
Than the virgin's meek demeanor.

In times which test the soul,
Lose yourself in revelry.
The elixir of pure being lends
The poorest soul the riches of Qarun.

Do not wax on in Pride
Or like the candle
Soon you'll melt
From the angry fire.
Even the diamond melts away
If near *this* flame it, too, should stray.

The wine glass is the Mirror
From within this ruby orb
Every secret is revealed;
The soul's attainment yet concealed.

Proclaim this news immediately:
Life comes from Beauties singing Farsi
To renegades residing in your country.

Hafez, himself donned not this wine streaked
And tattered cloak. Oh Sheik,
Of pure raiment, *forgive*, I beseech.

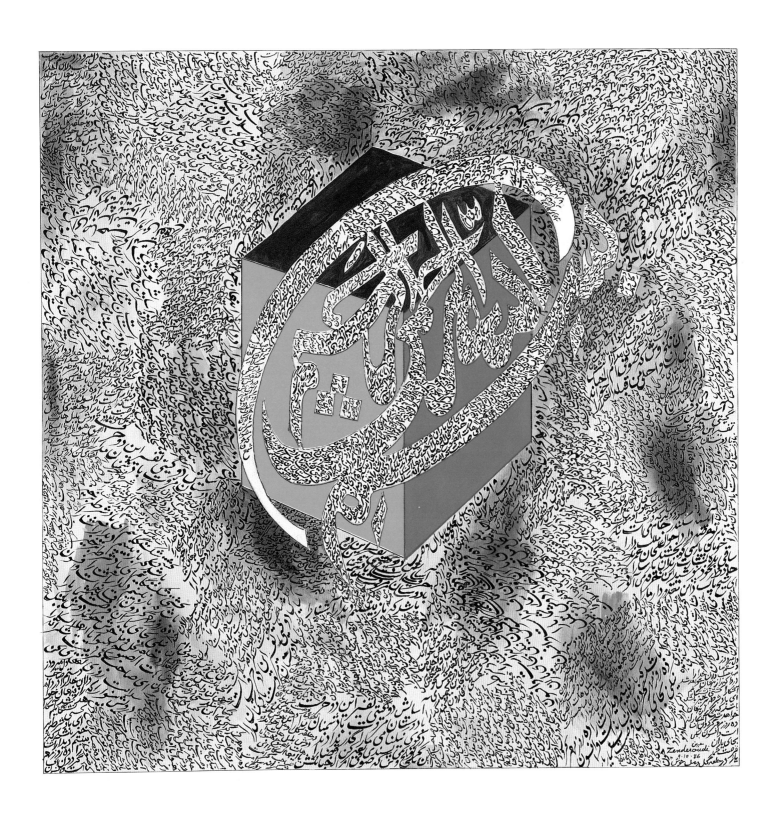

For God's sake come to my cry. O pious ones! forth from the hand, goeth my heart. For God's sake:
O the pain that the hidden mystery [of love] should be disclosed.

We are boat-stranded ones! O fair breeze! arise.
It may be that, again, we may behold the face of the Beloved.

For the [short] space of ten days, the sphere's favour is magic and sorcery:
O friend! regard as booty,—goodness in friends.

Last night in the assembly of the rose and of wine,—the bolbol sweetly sang:
O Saqi! give wine: O intoxicated ones! come to life!

O generous one! in thanks for thy own safety—
One day, make inquiry of the welfare of the foodless darvish.

The ease of two worlds is the explanation of these two words:—
With friends, kindness; with enemies, courtesy.

In the street of good name, they [Fate and Destiny] gave us no admission:
If thou approve not, —change our Fate.

That bitter wine, which the Sufi called—"The mother of iniquities,"
To us, is more pleasant and more sweet than the kisses of virgins.

In the time of straitedness, strive in pleasure and in intoxication:
For, this elixir of existence maketh the beggar [rich as] Karun.

Be not arrogant; for thee, like a candle, with wrath will consume,
The Heart-Ravisher in whose hand, the hard stone is [as] soft wax.

The cup of wine is Sekandar's mirror. Behold,—
So that it may show thee the state of Dara's kingdom [the soul].

Life-givers, are the lovely ones, Persian-prattling:
O Saqi! this news, give to the rends of Fars [Persia].

Of himself, Hafez put not on this patched, wine-stained garment
O shaikh, pure of skirt! hold us excused.

دل می‌رود ز دستم صاحبدلان خدا را   در دا که راز پنهان خواهد شد آشکارا

کشتی شکسته‌گانیم ای باد شرطه برخیز   باشد که باز بینم دیدارِ آشنا را

ده روزه مهر گردون افسانه است و افسون   نیکی بجای یاران فرصت شمار یا را

در حلقهٔ گل و مل خوش خواند دوش بلبل   هات الصبوح هبوا یا ایها السکارا

ای صاحب کرامت شکرانهٔ سلامت   روزی تفقدی کن درویش بی‌نوا را

آسایش دو گیتی تفسیر این دو حرف است   با دوستان مروت با دشمنان مدارا

در کوی نیکنامی ما را گذر ندادند   گر تو نمی‌پسندی تغییر کن قضا را

آن تلخ‌وش که صوفی امّ الخبائثش خواند   اشهی لنا و احلی من قبلة العذارا

هنگام تنگدستی در عیش کوش و مستی   کاین کیمیای هستی قارون کند گدا را

سرکش مشو که چون شمع از غیرتت بسوزد   دلبر که در کفِ او موم است سنگِ خارا

آیینهٔ سکندر جامِ می است بنگر   تا بر تو عرضه دارد احوال ملکِ دارا

خوبانِ پارسی‌گو بخشندگانِ عمرند   ساقی بده بشارت رندانِ پارسا را

حافظ به خود نپوشید این خرقهٔ می‌آلود   ای شیخ پاک‌دامن معذور دار ما را

The green fields of the sky I saw
Mowed with the sickle of the new moon.
I thought back to what I'd sown
And to the harvest, what it might draw.

And then I talked to Fortune,
"You've overslept. See, the sun's already risen."
He replied, "Don't despair,
With what you've done your record will repair."

If you go as Christ to the sky
Clothed in simple purity,
Then your light shall rise and become
As a hundred rays connect to the sun.

But do not rely upon the lunar star
He is a wayward rogue
Who lifted the crown of Kaus
And knicked the belt of Khusrau.

Though the ear strains
From the gold and ruby jewel,
Attend! Passing beauty shan't remain
So give yourself to counsel's rule.

God protect your mark of beauty
From the evil eye's effect.
By that beauty
The moon and sun are held in check.

Tell the sky not to
                    vaunt its beauty.
For in love the moon's harvest goes for but a grain of barley,
        And the Pleiades for two.

The fire of the hypocrite's sham show
Shall consume Faith's harvest.
Hafez, doff your woollen cloak
                    —and go!

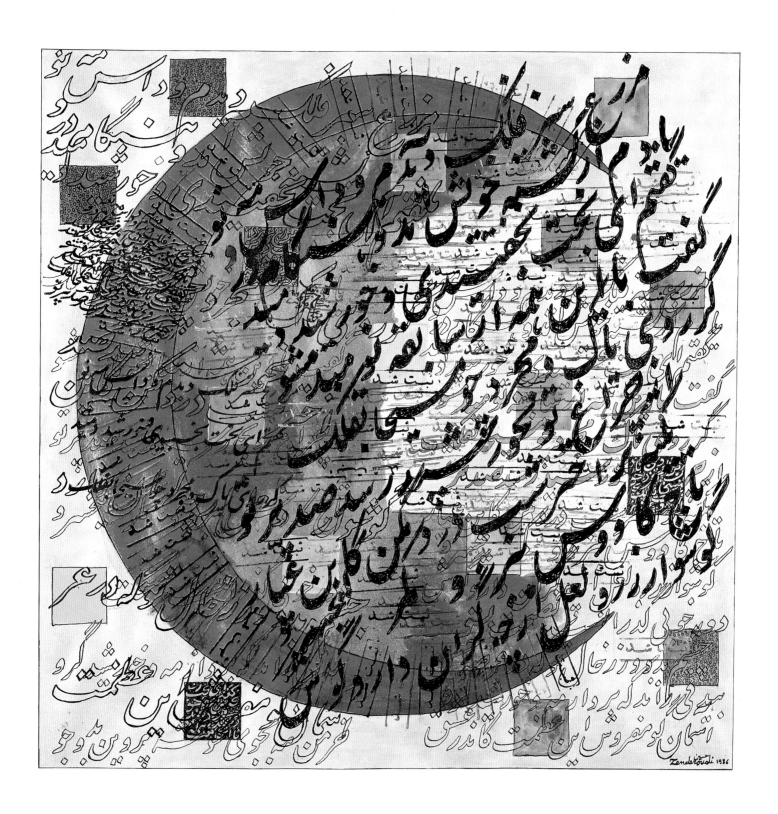

The green expanse of sky, I behold; and the sickle [the crescent] of the new moon;
To me, recollection came of my own sown-field; and of the time of reaping
[the judgement day].

I said:—"Oh fortune! thou hast slept; and appeared hath the sun:"
He said:—"Despite all this, hopeless of the past, be not."

If, like the Masiha [the anointed one], to the sky [heaven] thou go pure
and free [of the body],
To the sun, will reach many a ray of thy splendour.

On the star, the [wandering] thief of night,—rely not. For this knave
Took the crown of Kay Ka'us; and the girdle of Kay Khusrau.

Although the ear be heavy with [dull to] the ear-ring of gold and of ruby
[profitable counsel],
The season of beauteousness [youthfulness] is passing; counsel, hear.

From thy mole, far the evil eye! For, on the chess-board of beauty,
It [thy mole] moved a pawn that, from the moon and the sun [the moles of
the sky], the bet won.

Tell the sky:—"Boast not of this pomp. For, in love,
"[They sell] the moon's harvest [the halo] for a barley-corn; and the cluster
of the Pleiades for two barley-corns."

The fire of hypocrisy and deceit will consume the harvest of religion,
Hafez! this woollen kherqe, cast away; and go.

مَزرعِ سبزِ فلک دیدم و داسِ مه نو
یادم از کشتهٔ خویش آمد و هنگامِ درو

گفتم ای بخت بخفتیدی و خورشید دمید
گفت با این همه از سابقه نومید مشو

گر روی پاک و مجرّد چو مسیح از فلک
از چراغ تو به خورشید رسد صد پرتو

تکیه بر اخترِ شب دزد مکن کاین عیّار
تاجِ کاووس بِبُرد و کمرِ کیخسرو

گوشوارِ زر و لعل ارچه گران دارد گوش
دورِ خوبی گذرانست نصیحت بشنو

چشمِ بد دور ز خالِ تو که در عرصهٔ حُسن
بیدَقی راند که بُرد از مه و خورشید گرُو

آسمان گو مفروش این عظمت کاندر عشق
خرمنِ مه به جوی خوشهٔ پروین به دو جُو

آتشِ زهد و ریا خرمنِ دین خواهد سوخت
حافظ این خرقهٔ پشمینه بینداز و برو

Rendezvous

With mussed-up hair and moistened brow
The tempting lips of an intoxicated smile
With open blouse rent to the waist,
Singing a sonnet's soft strain
Her cup contained a potent brew.

With provocative glance and slanted smile
She came at midnight and sat awhile.
Then whispered in soft, low tones,
"Have you given way to sleep,
You who have been my faithful lover?"

Night watching lovers
Your love is a fake
If you don't pursue
The juice of this Grape.

Away, you hypocrites
Don't belittle those who drink of the cask,
Even the dregs can be dear,
For no more was given when creation was cast.

I have drunk to the end
What was given to me
Whether it came from the cask
Or the cup of Eternity.

How many, as Hafez, to repentance have resigned
By fetching billowed hair and heady flowing wine?

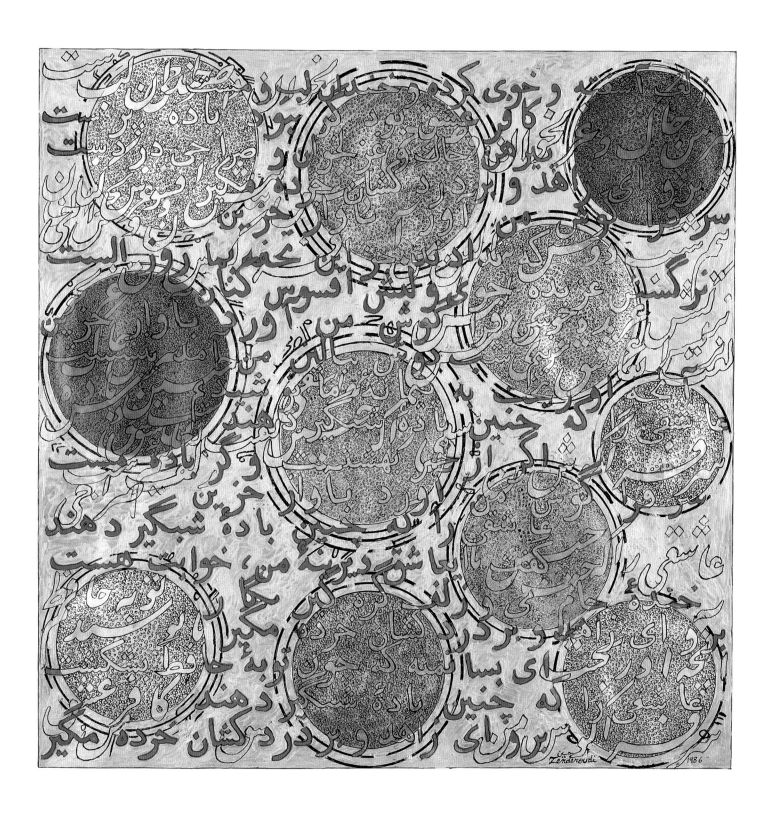

Tress dishevelled; sweat expressed; lip laughing; intoxicated;
Garment rent; song-singing; goblet in His hand;

Eye, contest-seeking; lip lamenting—
Came, at midnight, last night, to my pillow; [and there] sate.

To my ear, He brought His head; [and], in a low soft voice,
Said:—"Oh my distraught Lover! sleep is thine" [sleep hath overcome thee].

That ['Aref] Lover, to whom they give wine like this, night-watching
Is infidel to love, if he be not wine-worshipper.

Oh Zahed! go: seize not a small matter against the drinkers of wine-dregs:
For, save this gift [of dregs], naught did they give us on the day of Alast.

Of whatever, He [God] poured into our cup, we have drunk [good or bad];
Whether it be of the wine of Paradise, or of the cup of intoxication.

The laughter [of mantling foam] of the cup of wine; and the knot-seizing tress
of the Beloved—
O many a repentance, hath it shattered like the repentance of Hafez.

زلفْ آشفته و خوی کرده و خندان لب و مست

پیرهن چاک و غزل‌خوان و صراحی در دست

نرگسش عربده جوی و لبش افسوس کنان

نیم‌شب دوش به بالین من آمد بنشست

سر فرا گوش من آورد به آواز حزین

گفت ای عاشق دیرینه من خوابت هست

عاشقی را که چنین باده شبگیر دهند

کافر عشق بود گر نشود باده‌پرست

برو ای زاهد و بر دردکشان خرده مگیر

که ندادند جز این تحفه به ما روز الست

آنچه او ریخت به پیمانه ما نوشیدیم

اگر از خمر بهشتست و گر باده مست

خنده جام می و زلف گره گیر نگار

ای بسا توبه که چون توبه حافظ بشکست

Last night I shuffled to the tavern
With eyelids drooping
      Polluted
My robe was dripping;
Wine soaked my prayer rug
       Polluted.

The publican's young mage then chided,
"Wake up you sleepy voyager
Wash yourself and stagger
To this monastic door,
Or you will bring us ill—pollution."

In passion for your lover's lips
You defile your very soul
With the ruby's blood extolled.

Instead, pass your silver years purified.
Do not pollute the garments of age
Like those once worn in youth.

Not from Nature's well
Will purification come;
For this water will not remove the stain.

Then I said, "Oh World Soul it isn't wrong
That the new rose leaf find its purity
From the flowing ruby wine, polluted.

In Love's wide ocean
The sailors there
Were swallowed by the seas
But thereby not
      Polluted.

"Hafez," he said. "Don't fill your friends
With pedantic riddles."
Alas, these gentle words, full of reproach
In many ways
         Polluted.

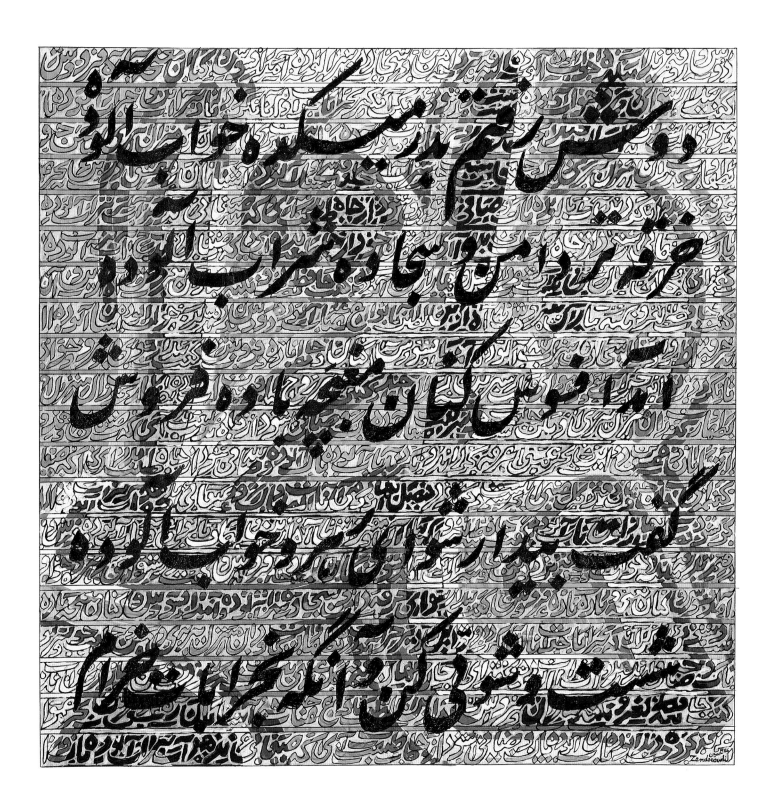

Last night, to the door of the wine-house, I went, sleep—stained.
The kherqe wet of skirt, and the prayer-mat, wine—stained.

The magian boy of the wine-seller, cry-making, came;
He said:—"Awake, O wayfarer, sleep—stained.

"Washing and washing, do; then, to the tavern, proudly move;
"So that, by thee, this ruined cloister become not—stained.

"In desire for those sweet of mouth [beloved ones], how long makest thou
"The jewel of thy soul with the melted ruby [the bloody tear]—stained?"

"In purity, pass the stage of old age; and make not,
"The honour-robe of old age, with the splendid dress of youth,—stained.

Pure and clean, be; and, from nature's well, come forth;
Giveth not purity water, earth—stained.

I said:—"O soul of the world! not a defect is it, the rose-book—
"If, in the spring season, it become with pure [ruddy] wine—bestained."

In this deep sea [of love] those acquainted with love's path,
Were drowned; and were not with water—stained.

He said:—"Hafez! to friends, thy jest and subtlety boast not;
"Alas for this [thy] grace, with varied forms of reproach—bestained."

دوش رفتم به در میکده خواب‌آلوده / خرقه تر دامن و سجاده شراب‌آلوده

آمد افسوس‌کنان مغبچهٔ باده‌فروش / گفت بیدار شو ای رهرو خواب‌آلوده

شست و شویی کن و آنگه به خرابات خرام / تا نگردد ز تو این دیر خراب‌آلوده

به هوای لب شیرین پسران چند کنی / جوهر روح به یاقوت مذاب آلوده

به طهارت گذران منزل پیری و مکن / خلعت شیب چو تشریف شباب آلوده

پاک و صافی شو و از چاه طبیعت به درآی / که صفایی ندهد آب تراب‌آلوده

گفتم ای جان جهان دفتر گل عیبی نیست / که شود فصل بهار از می ناب آلوده

آشنایان ره عشق در این بحر عمیق / غرقه گشتند و نگشتند به آب آلوده

گفت حافظ لغز و نکتهٔ به یاران مفروش / آه از این لطف به انواع عتاب آلوده

The Veil

Last night I saw the angels
Rapping at the tavern door.
The clay of Adam
In a bowl they kneaded and shaped.

The visitors from that secret realm of purity
Sat me down
On the dusty road
And poured me out a drink.

The consignment,
Which the sky could not bear,
The work of chance
Assigned to me, the fool.

The churches war among themselves.
Forgive them. They do not see the Truth.
To compensate they bicker and bluster
Over fairy tales.

Thanks be to God
That *our* schisms have been bridged.
Joyful Sufis sang and danced
And raised a toast of thanks.

The real fire is not in the flame
That dances on the candle wick
Observe the moths and where they gather:
For there the true beacon blazes.

The veil of Wisdom's Beauty uniquely by Hafez
Has been drawn—and through his songs
The bride of poetry's flowing locks lovingly he has groomed.

Last night I saw that the angels beat [at] the door of the tavern,
The clay of Adam, they shaped and into the mould, they—cast.

The dwellers of the sacred fold of the veiling and of the abstaining of the angels,
On me, dust-sitter, the intoxicating wine—cast.

The load of deposit, the sky could not endure:
In the name of helpless me, the dice of the work, they—cast.

The wrangle of seventy-two sects, establish excuse for all—
When truth, they saw not, the door of fable they—beat.

Thanks to God, between me and Him, peace chanced,
The cup of thankfulness, the Sufis, dancing,—cast.

Not fire is that, whereat the candle's flame laugheth:
Fire is that, wherein the moth's harvest [body] they—cast.

From off thought's face, none hath drawn the veil as Hafez [hath]
Since [the time when] the tress-tip, the brides of speech—combed.

دوش دیدم که ملایک درِ میخانه زدند   گِلِ آدم بسرشتند و به پیمانه زدند

ساکنانِ حرمِ سترّ و عفافِ ملکوت   با من راهنشین بادهٔ مستانه زدند

آسمان بارِ امانت نتوانست کشید   قرعهٔ کار بنامِ من دیوانه زدند

جنگِ هفتاد و دو ملّت همه را عذر بنه   چون ندیدند حقیقت رهِ افسانه زدند

شکر ایزد که میانِ من و او صلح افتاد   صوفیان رقص کنان ساغرِ شکرانه زدند

آتش آن نیست که از شعلهٔ او خندد شمع   آتش آنست که در خرمنِ من پروانه زدند

کس چو حافظ نگشاد از رخِ اندیشه نقاب   تا سرِ زلفِ سخن را به قلم شانه زدند

Back to the Heart

For years my heart sought the cup of Jamshid from me,
    What it had, the heart went pursuing
    From the stranger it was pursuing
Inner secrets of the sacred mysteries.

A pearl beyond the shell of space and time
    The pearl my heart was seeking
    The cup my heart was seeking
From those lost on the shore of brine.

Late last night I took my question
    To the elder Mage I went
    To solve the riddle I went
For his sight was from God's direction.

What I saw was great laughter and joy.
    With overflowing cup
    He stood there with the cup
That from within reflected a hundred mysteries.

I asked him then, "Please tell me when
    The Sage gave thee the cup?"
    He answered that the cup
Was presented on the day the Sage made heaven.

One searching heart was sorely grieving;
    Though in his heart—was God,
    His eye viewed not—God,
And so he cried to God while still concealing.

In contrast to Sorcery, let Wisdom conjure here.
    As the twisting staff of Moses
    In the glowing hand of Moses
Those very inner mysteries which we hold most dear.

Remember the friend whose claim divine,
    "I am the Truth," said he.
    "The secrets are mine," said he.
Gave up his life for revealing the sign.

If the Holy Spirit shall will the gift,
    Then others may be empowered
    With miracles be empowered
Like the Messiah the dead to lift.

"What purpose serves the chain of braids?" says me.
    Replied the Mage, "It's a complaint, Hafez,
    "From searching, Hafez,
"That comes from a heart full of frenzy."

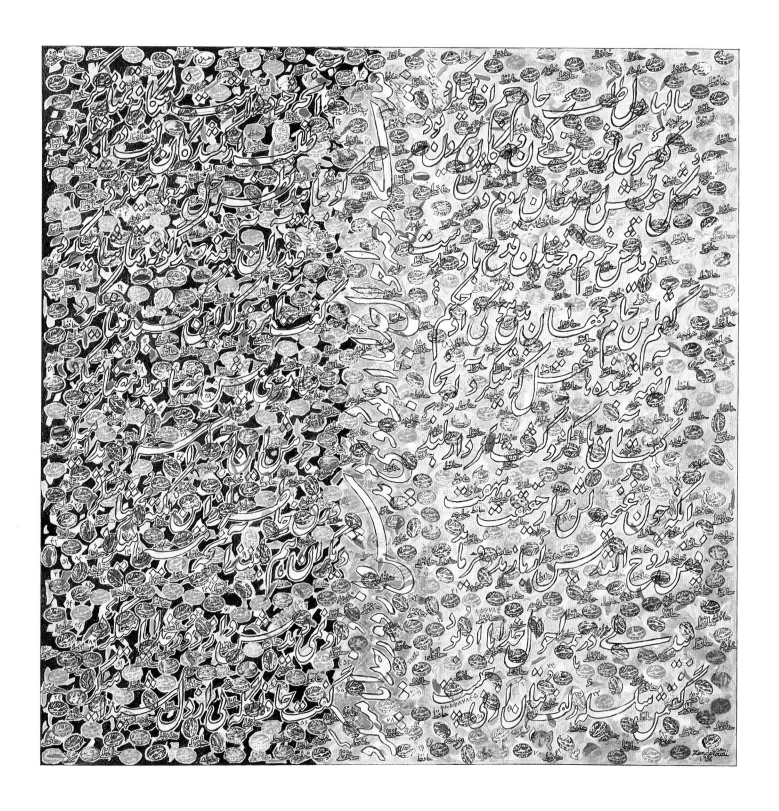

Search for the cup of Jamshid from me, years my heart—made.
And for what it [the cup] possessed, from a stranger, entreaty—made.

A jewel—that is beyond the shell of existence and of time,—
From those lost on the shore of the sea, search it [my heart]—made.

Last night, I took my difficulty to the Pir of the Magians,
Who, by strengthening of sight, the solving of subtlety—made.

Him, happy, laughing, wine-goblet in hand, I saw:
And in the mirror, a hundred kinds of views he—made.

I said:—"When gave the All-wise this cup world-viewing to thee?"
He said:—"On that day, when the azure dome [of heaven] He—made."

Our heart bereft,—with him, in all states, is God:
[But] he beheld Him not, and from afar [the cry]:—"For God's sake"—made.

All those sorceries that reason here made;
In the presence of the staff and of the white hand of Musa, Samiri—made.

He said:—"That friend [Hallaj], by whom lofty became the head of the gibbet,
"His crime was this: that clear, the mysteries of the sky, he—made."

If, again, the bounty of the Holy Spirit [Jibra'il] give aid,
Others also may make those [miracles], which the Masiha—made.

I said to him:—"The chain-like tress of idols is for the sake of what?"
He said:—"Of his own distraught heart, Hafez complaint—made."

سالها دل طلبِ جامِ جم از ما میکرد || وآنچه خود داشت ز بیگانه تمنّا میکرد

گوهری کز صدفِ کَون و مکان بیرون است || طلب از گمشدگانِ لبِ دریا میکرد

مشکلِ خویش برِ پیرِ مغان بردم دوش || کو به تأییدِ نظر حلِّ معمّا میکرد

دیدمش خرّم و خندان قدحِ باده به دست || و اندر آن آینه صد گونه تماشا میکرد

گفتم این جامِ جهان بین به تو کِی داد حکیم || گفت آن روز که این گنبدِ مینا میکرد

بیدلی در همه احوال خدا با او بود || او نمیدیدش و از دور خدا را میکرد

این همه شعبدهٔ خویش که میکرد اینجا || سامری پیشِ عصا و یَدِ بیضا میکرد

گفت آن یار کز او گشت سرِ دار بلند || جُرمش این بود که اسرار هویدا میکرد

فیضِ روحُ القدُس ار باز مدد فرماید || دیگران هم بکنند آنچه مسیحا میکرد

گفتمش سلسلهٔ زلفِ بتان از پیِ چیست || گفت حافظ گله‌ای از دلِ شیدا میکرد

From Behind the Caravan

Standing at the threshold without demanding the vainglory of Fame
    We have come.

Seeking a refuge from the cruel battering of Fortune
    We have come.

Traveling along love's journey,
From the borders of nothingness to states of being
    We have come.

Seeing that vital cenacle from the Garden of Paradise
In search of Love's greenery
    We have come.

Yearning for that most precious, guarded treasure
As humble supplicants to the door of the King
    We have come.

Pride and Honor are at stake; clouds release your purifying showers
For to a Sovereign Judge whose black book lies open
    We have come.

Hafez, throw off your overcoat!
It is with the breath of fire, behind the caravan,
    We have come.

Not in pursuit of pomp and of pageant, to this door—we have come:
For shelter from ill-fortune, here—we have come.

Way-farers of love's stage are we: and from the limits of non-existence,
Up to the climes of existence, all this way—we have come.

The freshness of your down, we saw; and, from the garden of paradise,
In search of this love-grass,—we have come.

With such treasure, whose treasurer is the faithful spirit,
In beggary to the door of the King's house—we have come.

O bark of grace! thy anchor of patience is where?
For, in this ocean of liberality, immersed in sin—we have come.

O cloud, sin-cleansing! honour goeth; [mercy] rain:
For in the court of action black of book,—we have come.

Hafez! this woollen kherqe [of outward worship] cast. For [with love's consuming and melting],
From behind the kafila with the fire of sighing [and wailing]—we have come.

ما بدین در نه پی حشمت و جاه آمده ایم / از بد حادثه اینجا به پناه آمده ایم

رهرو منزل عشقیم و ز سر حد عدم / تا به اقلیم وجود این همه راه آمده ایم

سبزه خط تو دیدیم و ز بستان بهشت / به طلب کاری این مهر گیاه آمده ایم

با چنین گنج که شد خازن او روح امین / به گدائی به در خانه شاه آمده ایم

لنگر حلم تو ای کشتی توفیق کجاست / که درین بحر کرم غرق گناه آمده ایم

آب رو می رود ای ابر خطا پوش ببار / که به دیوان عمل نامه سیاه آمده ایم

حافظ این خرقه پشمینه بینداز که ما / از پی قافله با آتش آه آمده ایم

TRANSLITERATIONS

AND NOTES

A guide for using the English alphabet to recite the poems in Persian

Poetry is music. Music is best appreciated when heard. The poems in this volume are no exception. The beauty of verbal sound patterns are most recognizable when recited.

For those readers who wish to have a go at the original, we have set forth some aids. These will facilitate an accurate facsimile of the poetry as recited today.

Now it should be noted that there is some controversy on some aspects of pronunciation. However, the following represents the conclusions of Dr. P.N. Khanlari in his studies, *Vazn-e She'r-e Farsi,* as well as his work with Vincent Monteil in French in 1952, and Elwell-Sutton's *The Persian Metres.*

The following transliterations in English script should help the Persian reader in accurate pronunciation and recitation. By the use of detailed phonetic symbols, some precision of expression can be achieved.

The rules are set out in this order:

    I. Vowels
        a. sounds
        b. connectives
    II. Consonants
        a. sounds
        b. connectives
    III. Rhythm
        a. meter
        b. accents
    IV. Putting it All Together: Hints on Reading

I. Vowels

  a. Sounds

	English	Persian
a	as	*nazar*
â	c*ar*	*Hâfez*
e	f*e*ll	*del*
î	plent*y*	*ravî*
ô	t*oe*	*jôhar*
û	S*ue*	*kû*

There are two diphthongs: *ey* and *ô.* The *ey* as in:

English: sail

Seyl-ē fanâ

The *ô* is normally oe, as in:

English: toe

Rah-Rô-ē manzel

b. Connectives

The annective particle (*ezâfe*) is always *-e* (or *-ye*, but never *i*) and can be short (*e*) or long (*ē*), according to the demands of the meter. It is toneless and supported by the previous word.

Nafas-ē bad-e

The joining liaison is also supported by the previous word and toneless, either short or long *ŏ* according to the demands of the meter (even after a vowel, but *yo* after *i*); in Persian it is never *-va*, *-vo* or *-ho*:

jân-o jahân

sobhi-yo

The preverb *be-* is often pronounced *bo-*, by assimilation with the vowel *o* of the following syllable:

be-gozarad > bo-gzarad

The final *i* is short in front of a vowel, but the following vowel (in the same phonetic word) is yodeled:

sobhi-yo

A long vowel followed by an *n* is considered short (as if the *n* did not count), except if the *n* is followed by another vowel:

xăndăn-lab, yărăn

qazal-xăn-o

II. Consonants

The consonants are less troublesome than the vowels.

Many Persian letters (four in the case of *z*) transcribe the same Persian sound.

(') indicates a hamzé, an 'eyn, or a glottal stop. And the *ghâf* and *gheyn* are both represented by *q*.

a. Sounds

x ....kh   (as in Scottish Lo*ch* Ness — *xandân*)

The cedilla is used in the following manner:

ş ....sh   (as in English *sharp* — *şod*)

| ç | .... tch | (as in English *champ* — *hamço*) |
| ẓ | .... zh | (as in English *vision* — *moẓde*) |

b. Connectives

— : a combination of the same grammatical and phonetic units tied together in meaning and pronounced together:

Ne-mî-dîd-aṣ-o

French: *C'est-à-dire* . . .
English: Not-to-say-that . . .

◡ : two words grouped together which normally do not go together in meaning or pronunciation, but which should in the poem be sounded together—usually the second word starts with a vowel:

be-bâq, ậmad

French: *S'en va, o nuage*
English: Illinois' election

III. Rhythm

The rhythm of Hafez's poetry is, as with all Persian poetry, based on the distinction of long and short syllables. One long is a little longer than two shorts.

Hafez principally used four different rhythms. But his favorite meter is the *ramal*, with an initial short syllable.

Nă-fă/-s-ē bâ//-d-ĕ să/-bâ mōṣ//-kˇ fĕ/-ṣâ(n) xâ//-hăd/ṣōd

a. Meter

The table below shows the composition of the short, long, and very long (—◡); these end in a furtive (ə), which counts as a short, and their role is important for achieving the correct meter.

— {	c + v̄	(*bâ*)
	c + v + c	(*bar*)
◡	c + v	(*be*)
—◡ {	c + v̄ + c	(*bazˀ*)
	c + v + c + c	(*bastˀ*)

b. Symbols of Emphasis

The music of Hafez's poetry plays on the whole range of vocal tones. The emphasis, however, which falls on certain syllables is very important. For simplification we have used only two marks. These marks (') (') denote the location and degree of emphasis. The location of this emphasis is important, because one word can have different meanings, depending on the syllable on which the emphasis falls. For example:

màrdî .... a man, and *mardî́* .... manliness

dùsti .... a friend, and *dustî́* .... friendship

In reciting Persian poetry, the emphasis is not as much an increase in volume as in pitch. This mark (') controls only the vowel on which it is placed. The bold mark (**'**), however, denotes greater emphasis in volume and pitch, primarily upon the whole word and secondarily on the syllable indicated. For example:

Qadàmî neh, be-vedå'-aş, ke ravån kâhad-şod!

IV. Putting it All Together: Hints on Reading

Even the greatest Persian scholars cannot pick-up an unknown Hafez poem and recite it perfectly. It requires practice!

What are some of the factors which will help make the process easier? Well, for one, putting some time into mastering each line. These phonetic notes should be of use here. The calligraphy of the poem should stand as notes of music to a musician. They point to the way, but do not exhaustively instruct. Within certain prelimitations are vast expanses of possible expression. The first bars of Beethoven's Fifth Symphony are among the best known in all of music—and yet look at the endless variation between the interpretations of Klemperer and Solti, for example. It is the same with poetic recitation. After some basic rules are met, there is ample room for individual interpretation.

This is the stage in which the poem becomes one's own: when one has it *par coeur*. It is at this point that the endless possibilities of good poetry open up to the patient reader.

Enjoy its petals when it is here
As soon as it comes it is gone.

Notes

In the notes, the numbers indicate lines and/or stanzas referred to within the poem.

Some lines from poems by Hafez's predecessors which may have inspired him are handwritten in Persian and included in the note margins. Other lines from Hafez's *Divan* reference his use of certain words.

Although in Clarke's translations we have removed most of the parenthetical interpolations included within the poems, we have nonetheless left those notes found to be interesting.

1. ***Moshk*** means musk. And although today it might not be associated with the perfume of a spring breeze, in the time of Hafez it was considered a sweet-smelling fragrance. Marco Polo writes in his travels to China, "In this country is found the best musk in the world, and I will tell you how it is produced. There exists in that region a kind of wild animal like a gazelle . . . when the creature has been taken, they find at the navel, between the flesh and the skin, something like an imposthume filled with blood, which they cut out and remove, with all the skin attached to it; and the blood inside this imposthume is the musk that produces that powerful perfume."

6. ***Sha'ban*** is the month before the month of fasting, ***Ramazan***. Although a devout Muslim must fast throughout the month from sunrise to sunset, *Ramazan* was not, necessarily, considered a month of harsh discipline (particularly for the rich). For although the days were spent in fasting, the evenings were an excuse to celebrate and party. Amongst the upper classes, this would result in celebrating all night and sleeping most of the day.

8. **Poetry and Song:** Persian literature developed, from its inception, in verse because it was to entertain in the popular modes of song or storytelling. The established meter and rhyme of the verse lines provided a succession of self-contained propositions that greatly helped the author or rhapsodist to recite from memory.

9. **Hafez** was a title given to those who could recite the Qor'an by heart and was used by the poet as his pen name (*takhalus*). He was also given two other titles: "the Tongue of the Invisible" (*Lesan'al qeyb*) and "the Interpreter of Mysteries" (*Tarjuman'al asrar*).

Clarke

2. The cup of the ***arghavan*** (the Syrtis or Judas tree) is its red blossom.

3. *Bolbol* is a nightingale.

Nă-fǎ/-s-ē bẫ//-d-ĕ sǎ/-bã moş̄//k³ fĕ/-şẫ(n) xẫ//-hãd/şod

Nafás-ē bấd-e sabâ moşk³-feşấn xâhad şod;
âlấm-ē pîr³, degar bâre, javấn xâhad şod.

Arqavân, jấm-e aqîqî, be-saman xâhad-dâd;
çáşm-e narges, be şaqâyeq, negarấn xâhad şod.

În tatâvol ke keşîd, az qấm-e hejrân, bolbol,
tâ sarâ-pardé-ye gol, na′re-zanấn xâhad şod.

Gar, ze-masjed, be-xarâbât şodam, xorde má-gîr:
majlés-ē va′z³ derâz-ast-o zamấn xâhad şod!

Ey del, ar eşrát-e emrûz³ be-fardâ fekanî,
mâyé-yē náqd-e baqấ-râ, ké zamấn xâhad şod?

Mâh-e şa′bân máneh az dast qadah, k-în xorşid
az nazar, tâ şab-e eyd-ē ramazấn, xâhad şod.

Gol azîz-ast³; qanîmat şomoríd-aş sohbat!
ke, be-bâq, âmad az-în rấh-o az-ấn xâhad şod . . .

Motrébâ! majlés-e óns-ast; qazal xấn-o sorûd:
çánd gûî, ke çonîn ráft-o çenấn xâhad şod?

Hâfez, az báhr-e to, âmad sǔ-ye eqlîm-e vojûd:
qadámî neh, be-vedấ′-aş, ke ravấn xâhad şod!

2. In the Persian there is a play on the words *dagh* and *banafshe*. *Dagh* means hot and also the (violet) scar of a burn. *Dagh* also symbolizes mourning from its relationship to *dakhme*, meaning cemetery, from the days when corpses were burnt. Today Zoroastrians continue to call their "Tower of Silence" *Dakhme*.

6. In the English verse translation, the Persian word *bot*, meaning idol, has been translated as "sun." The Persian word probably comes from Buddha, although in the time of Hafez, it was a word used to symbolize beauty, usually that of an adolescent boy. See "Rendezvous: Notes," page 80.

Clarke

2. Out of respect of the dark tress, it is said that the tomb becometh the dark violet bed.

4. The word "thee" refereth to "the crowd of griefs."

Tŏ hām/-çŏ sōb/-hĭ-yŏ/mān şām//-'-ē xāl/-vă-t-ē/să-hă/-r-ām

To, hamço sȯbhi-yo man, şȧm'-e xalvȧt-ē sahȧr-am;
tabassȯmî kon-o jȧn bîn-ke çȯn hȧmî sepȧr-am!

Çonȋn-ke, dar-dėl-e man, dȧq-e zȯlf-e sarkėş-e to-st,
banafşe-zȧrᵓ şavad torbȧt-am, ço dȧr-gozaram.

Bar-âsᵓ tȧn-e morȧd-at, goşâdė-am dȧr-e çeşm,
ke yėk nazar fekanî; xod fekȧndî az-nazȧr-am . . .

Çė şokrᵓ guyȧm-at, ey xėyl-e qam, afȧk Ȧllâh!
ke rȗz-e bî-kasî, âxar, nė-mî-ravî ze-sȧr-am.

Qolȧm-e mardȯm-e çėşm-am, ke, bâ-siȧhᵓ-delî,
hezȧrᵓ qatre bė-bârad, ço dȧrd-e dėl şemar-am.

Be-hȧr-nazar, bȯt-e mâ jelvė mî-konad, lȋkan,
kas, în kereşme nȧ-bînad, ke mȧn hamî negȧr-am.

Be-xȧk-e Hȧfez, agar yârᵓ bȯ-gzarad, çon bâd,
ze-şȯqᵓ, dar-dėl-e ân tangᵓnâ, kafȧn be-dar-am!

1. Ruzbehan Baqli, the visionary from Shiraz (died 1209), cites a *hadis*, "the red rose is the glory even of God" (Louis Massignon, Opera Minora).

5. *Parde* (Anglo-Indian Purdah) means "curtain" or "screen." It is the age-old reference to the screen behind which things are hidden.

6. The Persian word *tufân*, means "storm" and may come from the Chinese *tai-fung* (big wind).

9. The word *raqib* means "guardian." When two lovers both wish to guard the same thing, they become rivals, hence the meaning of *raqib* as "rival."

Clarke

1. See the Qor'an, xciv.
   Kolbe-ye ahzan (the sorrowful cell) signifies: a distressed family.

Yû-sŏ/-f-ē gōm// gāş-tĕ/bâ-z ā̃//-yād bĕ/Kān-'ā̃n// qām mă/xōr

Yûsŏf-ē gom-gaşte bâz-âyad be Kan'ân.

          (Qam mȧ-xor. . . !)

Kolbė-yē ahzân şavad, rŭzî, golestân.

          (Qam mȧ-xor. . . !)

Ey dėl-ē qam-dîde, hȧl-at bėh şavad; del bad mȧ-kon!
v-în sȧr-ē şûrîde bâz-âyad be-sâmân.

          (Qam mȧ-xor. . . !)

Gar bahȧr-ē omrᵒ bâşad, bâzᵒ, bar tȧxt-ē çaman,
çȧtr-e gol, dar-sȧr keşî, ey mȯrq-e xoş-xân!

          (Qam mȧ-xor. . . !)

Dȯr-e gardûn, gar, do-rŭzî, bar-morȧd-e mâ nȧ-raft:
dâ'eman yėk-sân nȧ-bâşad, hȧl-e dȯrân.

          (Qam mȧ-xor. . . !)

Hân, mȧ-şŏ nômîdᵒ, çon vâqef nė-î az-sėrr-e qeyb:
bâşad, andar parde, bâzîhȧ-ye penhân.

          (Qam mȧ-xor. . . !)

Ey del, ar sëyl-ē fanâ, bonyȧd-e hastî bar-kanad,
çon tȯ-râ Nȗh-ast kaştî-bân: ze-tûfȧn

              qam mȧ-xor. . . !

Dar-biâbân, gar, be-şȯq-ē Ka'be, xâhȋ zad qadam,
sar-zaneş-hâ, gar konad xȧr-ē moqîlân,

              qam mȧ-xor. . . !

Garçė manzel bas xatarnȧk-ast-o maqsad bas ba'îd:
hîçᵒ rȧhî nîst k-ȧn-râ nîst pâyân.

          (Qam mȧ-xor. . . !)

Hȧl-e mâ, dar-forqȧt-ē jânȧn-o ebrȧm-ē raqîb,
jomlė mî-dânad Xodȧ-ye hȧlᵒ-gardân.

          (Qam mȧ-xor. . . !)

Hâfėzâ! dar-kȯnj-e fȧqr-ō xalvȧt-ē şabhȧ-ye târ,
tâ bovad vėrd-at do'ȧ-ō dȧrs Qor'ân:

              qam mȧ-xor. . . !

يوسف گم گشته بازآيد بکنعان غم مخور
اى دل غمديده حالت به شود دل بد مکن
کبار عمر باشد باز بر تخت چمن
دور گردون گر دو روزى بر مراد ما نرفت
هان مشو نوميد چون واقف نه اى از سر غيب
اى دل ار سيل فنا بنياد هستى بر کند
در بيابان گر بشوق کعبه خواهى زد قدم
گرچه منزل بس خطرناک است و مقصد بس بعيد
حال ما در فرقت جانان و ابرام رقيب
حافظ در کنج فقر و خلوت شبهاى تار

This *ghazal* is written on Hafez's tomb.

Wine drinking: "It is their custom to deliberate about the gravest matters when they are drunk; and what they approve in their counsels is proposed to them the next day . . . when they are now sober, and if being sober they still approve it, they act thereon, but if not, they cast it aside (bk I.133)."

This is what Herodotus said of the Persians of the Achaemenean period. And long after the advent of Islam, the tradition of wine-drinking continued in Persian courts.

Sâqi **(Wine-server):** "The wine was usually served by young slaves. The full training of a boy slave included horsemanship, handling arms, marksmanship, and also serving wine at drinking banquets. According to Nizam al-Mulk, a properly educated slave was taught to serve wine in the sixth year of his training. At their best, such slaves were excellent soldiers and fine horsemen, played a musical instrument, were refined in their manners, and proved delightful companions, as amply attested by the poetry of the period. Some could even engage in discussions on highly specialized literary techniques.

"In Persian poetry, they were frequently dubbed as 'Turk.' Not that all these youths came from Turkistan, but the best types were reputed to come from that area. They were noted for both their good appearance and their bravery as soldiers." (Yarshater, 1960)

4. The Persian word *bu*, meaning perfume or fragrance, often refers to "desire." The direct relationship between perfume and sexual desire is, of course, well-known.

Mŏẓ-dĕ/yē vās//-l-ĕ tŏ/kŭ k-āz//să-r-ĕ/jã(n) bār// x̆ĩ̄/-zam

Moẓdė-yē vȧsl-e to kû, k-az-sȧr-e jản bar-xîzam?
tâyėr-ē qȯds-am-o az-dảm-e jahản bar-xîzam.

Be-valả-yē to, ke gar bandė-ye xîṣ-am xânî,
az-sȧr-ē xâjegȯ-yē kȯn-o makản, bar-xîzam.

Yâ Rab, az-ȧbr-e hedâyat bė-rasân bârảnî,
pîṣᵓtȧr z-ân-ke, ço gȧrdî, ze-miyản bar-xîzam.

Bar-sȧr-ē torbȧt-e man, bâ-mėy-o motreb, bė-neşîn,
tâ, be-bủy-at, ze-lahad, rȧqsᵓ-konản, bar-xîzam!

Xȋz-o bâlả be-namâ, ey bȯt-e şîrȋn-harakât,
k-az-sȧr-ē jản-o jahân, dastᵓ-feşản, bar-xîzam.

Garçė pîr-am, to, şȧbî, tangᵓ, dar-âqủş-am, keş,
tâ, sahar-gah, ze-kenảr-ē to, javản bar-xîzam!

Rủz-e mȧrg-am, nafȧsî, mohlȧt-e dîdảrᵓ be-deh,
tâ, ço Hâfez, ze-sȧr-ē jản-o jahản, bar-xîzam!

4. **Mogh-bache** (Magian child) is translated in the English verse as Mage child. Mage is the Old English form of the Greek "Magus" used to refer to the Persian word *Mogh* (possibly from the sanskrit word *Maghâ*, which means riches, gratuity, bounty, and giving). The Magi were members of the ancient Persian priestly caste of a Median tribe. It was the cross-fertilization of Zoroaster's teachings from eastern Iran [India] with the established network of these Median Priests (central-northern Iran, Hamadan) that produced the quick spread of Zoroastrianism throughout Persia in the 4th and 5th centuries B.C.E. Because of these priests' heavy emphasis on ritual, the Greeks used the term Magus to refer to those skilled in Oriental magic and astrology, from which comes the English word "magic."

After the advent of Islam, the taverns (*meykhâne*) were run by Zoroastrians since Muslims were not permitted such an occupation. The poets of this period turned the tavern into a sacred place, and gave the tavern-keeper the title of a Sage, *Pir-e Moghan* (Magian Elder), and called his helper *Mogh-bache* (Magian Child).

10. **Rend**, or the act of *rendi*, cannot be translated by any single word in English. In the dictionary it is variously defined as: drunkard, rogue, a deceiving, cunning, bold renegade. The word seems to have appeared in the 12th century and for the historians it meant a ruffian. The poets, however, often used it synonymously for the *Qalandar*, a minority sect who were said to shun all polite forms and habits of society, and to reject all rules. They had nothing to do with asceticism, nor with renouncing the things of this world, nor with living poorly. The only thing they were concerned with was their internal serenity and the purity of their hearts toward God.

Clarke

1. *Raunagh* (splendour) signifies: the opening of the path of Truth.

2. *Sabâ* (breeze) signifies: the holy traveller, perfect in companionship, fellow in breath, fellow in spirit.
   Javanân-e chaman (youths of the meadow) signifies: those who have gained access to the court of the Eternal.

6. *Mardân-e-khodâ* signifies: men of God, without how and why.
   Kashti-e-Nuh signifies: the world which, like Noah's ark, is immersed in the deluge of disaster.

9. *Mâh-e-Kan'ân* may signify:
   (a) Yusuf.
   (b) the heart of Hafez.

12. *mey* signifies: love, perfect of test.
   rendi (profligacy) signifies: concealing mysteries beneath one's own veil; or choosing perfect peace. That is—grieving for none, and none grieving.
   Tazvir signifies: deceit.

Rō-nă/-qē aḥd//-ĕ ṣa/bāb āst//ⁱ dĕ/-gar bōs//tᾱn/-rᾱ

Rônaq-ē ahd-e ṣabâb-ast degar bostân râ
Mi-rasad moẕde-ye gôl, bolbol-e xoṣ al-hân râ.

Ey sabâ, gar be javânân-e çaman bâzᵊ rasi,
Xedmat-ē mâ berasân, sarv-o gol-o reyhân râ.

Gar çŏnin jelve konad moq-baçe-yē bâde-forûṣ,
Xâkᵊ-rub-ē dar-e meyxâne konam moẕgân râ.

Ey, ke bar mah keṣi az anbar-e sârâ çôgân;
Moztareb-hâl ma-gardân, man-e sargardân râ.

Tarsam, in qôm ke bar dord-keṣân mi-xan-dand,
Dar sar-ē kâr-e xarâbât konand, imân râ.

Yâr-e mardân-e, xodâ bâṣᵊ, ke dar kaṣti-ye Nûh,
Hast xâki ke be-âbi naxarad tufân râ.

Boro az xâne-ye gardûn be-dar-o, nân matalab;
K-ân siyah kâse, dar âxar be-koṣad mehmân râ.

Har ke ra xâbgah-ē âxar, moṣti, xâk, ast;
Gu, çĕ hâjat ke be-aflâk keṣi eyvân râ.

Mâh-e kan′âni-ye man, masnad-e mesr ân-e to ṣod;
Vaqt-ē ân-ast ke bedrud koni zendân râ.

Hâfezâ, mey xor-o rendi kon-o xoṣ bâṣ vali,
Dâm-e tazvir makon çon degarân Qor′ân râ.

Boatpeople

Clarke

2. *Bad-e short'e* (the favourable wind).

5. *Saheb keramat* (One possessed of liberality).

8. *Talkhvash* (bitter) signifies: (a) the wine of poverty, or of patience and endurance; (b) (bitter) counsel; or (c) wine whose drinker becometh intoxicated.
   Qoblat (a kiss) signifies: a kiss on the face of a pure one (a virgin).
   In his *Bustan*, Sa'di saith:
   "It is a crime to give sugar to the sick one,
    For whom, the bitter medicine is fit."

9. Qarun (Korah), the son of Yashar (Izhar), the uncle of Musa (Moses), was the handsomest and richest man of the men of Isra'il. He had a large palace, overlaid with gold; furnished with doors of massive gold.
   One day, when Musa declared to the people that adulterers should be stoned, he asked: "What if you should be found guilty of the crime?"
   Musa replied: "I should suffer the same punishment."
   Thereupon Karun produced a harlot who publicly charged him.
   Musa adjuring her to speak the truth, she at length confessed that she had been suborned by Karun.
   Then God directed Musa to command the Earth what he pleased.
   Whereupon he said: "Oh Earth swallow them up!"
   Immediately, the Earth opened, and swallowed Karun, his confederates, his palace, and all his riches.
   As Karun sank into the ground he cried out four times: "O Musa spare me!"
   But Musa kept saying: "Oh Earth, swallow them up!"
   God then said to Musa: "Thou hadst no mercy on Karun, though he asked pardon of thee four times. Had he asked me but once, I would have spared him."
   See The Bible, Numbers xvi.; the Qor'an, xxviii, 76.

10. Of the Arch-Angel, Mikail, Mohammad asked: "Speaketh God in Persian?"
   The Arch-Angel replied: "Yes: He saith: 'What shall I do with this handful of tyrants, save to forgive them?' "
   The grace of *parsi* and *parsa* should be noted.

11. If *Jâm-e-Jam* be read for *jâm-e-mai*, *Jâm-e-Jam* signifies: the heart of the *Aref*.
   Dara signifies: (a) love for the possessor of divine knowledge (the *Aref*); or (b) the soul (*nafs*).
The first line will be:
   Sekandar's (Alexander's) mirror (the heart) to the cup of Jamshid (world-displaying), behold.
   As long as the cup, like the cup of Jamshid, is the revealer of the mystery of time and of Earth, for Sekandar's mirror (that revealed the circumstances of the land of Dara) is the heart of the *Aref* (our *murshed*), at it, glance so that the mysteries of Love may for thy sake be revealed; and naught from thee, concealed.

Dēl mĭ-rɒ̆//vɒd zĕ dɒs-tɒm,//sɒ̃-hēb-dĕ-//lɑ̃n xŏ-dɒ̃-rɒ̄

Del mĭravad ze dastam, sâheb-delân xodâ râ;
Dắrd-â ke râz-e penhân, xâhad° şod âşkâ râ.

Kaşti-şekastegân-im, ey bắd-e şort-e bar-xiz
Bâşad ke bâz binam didâr-e âşna râ.

Dah rûz-e mehr-e gardûn afsane ast-o afsûn;
Niki be jâ-ye yârân forsat şomâr°, yâr-â.

Dar halqe-ye gôl-o môl, xŏş xând° dûş° bolbol.
Hât el-sabuh hob-bu ya ayyoha assokârâ.

Ey sắheb-ē kerâmat, şokrâne-yē salâmat,
Rûzi tafaqqodi-kon darviş-e bi-navâ râ.

Âsâyeş-ē do giti tafsir-e in do harf-ast:
Bâ dûstân morov'at, bâ doşman-ân modârâ.

Dar kûy-e nik°-nâmi, mârâ gozar nadâd-and;
Gar to nemi-pasandi, taq-yir° kon qazâ râ.

Ân talx vaş ke sûfi, omm'al xabâ-es-aş xând
Aş hâ la-nâ va ahlâ men qobla-tel azâ râ.

Hengâm-e tang dastî, dar eyş kush-o masti;
K-in kimi-ya-ye hasti, Qârun konad gedâ-râ.

Sarkeş mắş-o ke çon şam', as qeyrat-at besûzad;
Delbar ke dar kaf-e û, mûm-ast° sang-e xârâ.

Âyene-yē Sekandar jâm-ē mếy-ast°, bengar;
Tâ-bar to arzế dârad, ahvâl-e molk-e Dârâ.

Xûbân-e pârsi gu, baxşande-gân-e ốmr-and;
Sâ'qi, bedế beşârat, rendân-e Pârsâ râ.

Hâfez be-xŏd na-puşid, în xerqe-ye mey, âlûd.
Ey şếyx-e pâk°-dâman, ma'zûr° dâr° mâ râ.

The first complete manuscript of Hafez's poetry is said to have been written 35 years (1424) after his death. Two Hafez scholars, M. Qazvini and Dr. G. Ghani, used this manuscript and three others as the basis for their revised and corrected text originally published in 1941. Although this edition has been the most widely accepted, it is no longer considered by scholars as the sole foundation for the text of Hafez. Another later study by P.N. Khanlari compares various manuscripts, including some very early incomplete manuscripts written from 16 to 33 years after Hafez's death. We have included some of these variations in the notes.

Hafez may have written down different versions of the same poem for different audiences or occasions.

2. *Sâbeqe* means past record, but mystics use it to refer to the initial compassion of God.

3. Contrary to the Christian belief of the crucifixion, the Qor'an says (iv.155) ''. . . yet they [Jews] did not slay Him [Christ], neither crucified Him, only a likeness was shown to them . . . God raised Him up to Him . . .'' In Persian, *Masih* (Messiah) continues to mean ''annointed'' (by God).

Each of the seven quadrants of the sky has a star and a prophet. The sun and Christ are both in the fourth quadrant.

4. Kavous (Kaus) and Chosroe (Khusrau) were ancient Persian kings.
''The star, the thief of night'' signifies: the moon.

8. Some old manuscripts substitute *zohd-e riya* (prayer of deceit) for *zohd-o riya* (prayer and deceit).

Mǎz-rǎ/-ʾē sāb//-z-ĕ fǎ/-lāk̇ dǐ//-dǎ-m-ŏ/dâ-s-ē//mǎ-h-ĕ/nõ

Mazrȧ′-ē sȧbz-e falak dǐdam-o dȧ́s-ē mȧh-e nô:
yȧ́d-am az-keştė́-ye xîş âmȧ́d-o hengȧ́m-e derô.

Gȯ́ftam: ''Ey baxtᵊ, bė-xoftîdi-yo xorşîdᵊ damîd!''
Goftᵊ: ''Bâ-în-hame, az-sâbeqe, nômîdᵊ mȧ́-şô!''

Gar ravî, pȧ́k-o mojarrad, ço Masîhâ be-falak:
az-çerȧ́q-ē to, be-xorşîdᵊ, rasad sad partô!

Takye bar axtȧr-e şab-dozdᵊ mȧ́-kon, k-în ayyâr
tȧ́j-e Kâvûsᵊ be-bord-ō kamȧr-ē Key-Xosrô!

Gûsᵊ vȧr-ē zȧ́r-o laʾl, ar-çė́ gerân dârad gûş,
dȯr-e xûbî gozarȧ́n-astᵊ: nasîhat bė́-şenô!

Çė́şm-e bad, dȯ̊rᵊ ze-xȧ́l-ē to! ke, dar arsė́-ye hosn,
beydȧ́qî rândᵊ, ke bord, az-mȧ́h-o xorşîdᵊ, gerô.

Âsemȧ́n gû: ''mȧ́-forȯ̊ş în azamat! k-andar eşq:
xarmȧ́n-ē mah, be-jȯ́î; xûşė́-ye parvîn, be-dȯ́ jô!''

Âtȧ́ş-ê zȯhd-o riyâ, xarmȧ́n-e dîn xâhad sûxt;
Hâfez, în xerqė́-ye paşmîne bȋ́-yandâz-o bȯ́-rô!

Rendezvous

The Beloved: in the English verse translation, the beloved has become a woman. It should be noted that in the Persian poetry of this period the beloved is often a personalized concept and not an individual person and, as a rule, not a woman but a man. See "Dance of Life: Notes," page 72.

1. The origins of the *ghazal* as a poetic form are not known exactly (*ghazal* stems from the Arabic word "to make love" or "lovers' exchange"). Some say it comes from the erotic prelude (*nasib*) of the classic Arabic ode, while others take its origins to the pre-Islamic lyric poems (*cham*, later *chame*) recited in the courts of ancient Persia.

Although the *ghazal* has often been called an ode in English translation, it is actually much closer to the sonnet. Even in their development, the *ghazal* and the English sonnet have much in common. In fact, we suggest that the sonnet developed in Italy as a result of Arabic transmission of the *ghazal*. The 13th century poets of Italy were influenced by the love poetry of provençal troubadours, who were singing in southern Europe, in a time and place bubbling with the influence of Persian culture.

2. *Narges* (Narcissus) is used frequently by Hafez to mean the eye of the loved one.

The Persian word *afsus* today means "regret," but there is an older sense meaning "mockery."

5. *Zâhed* means sanctimonious ascetic.

Zŏl-fᵊ/'ā̆-ṣŏf//-tĕ-ŏ/xōy kār//-dĕ-ŏ/xān-dān//lă-b-ŏ/mă̄s(t)

Zolfᵊ-'âşofte̊-o xoy-karde̊-o xandân-låb-o mast,
pîrᵊhan çåk-o qazal-xån-o sorâhi̊ dar dast,

Narge̊s-aş arbade-jůy-o låb-aş afsůs-konân,
ni̊mᵊ-şab dûşᵊ, be-bâli̊n-e man, âmad be̊-neşast;

Sar farâ gůş-e man âvård-o be-âvâ̊z-e hazîn
goftᵊ: "Ey âşe̊q-e dîrîne̊-ye man, xåb-at hast? . . ."

Âşe̊qî-râ, ke çonîn bâde̊-ye şab-gîrᵊ dahand,
kâfår-ē e̊şqᵊ bovad, gar nå-şavad bâde-parast!

Bo̊-rô, ey zåhed-o bar do̊rdᵊ-kaşân, xorde må-gîr!
ke nå-dâdandᵊ, joz în tohfe, be-mâ, rûz-e alast!

Ânçe û rîxtᵊ be-peymâne̊-ye mâ, nûşi̊dim,
agar az xåmr-e beheşt åst-o gar az bâde̊-ye mast . . .

Xande̊-ye jåm-e me̊y-o zo̊lf-e gere-gîr-e negâr,
ey basâ tôbe, ke çon tôbe̊-ye Hâfez, be̊-şekast!

1. Taverns, *meykade* or *meykhâne*, were decrepit and disreputable places where wine and drugs were served. Thus the poet calls them *kharâbât* (ruins) but turns them into a sacred place for lovers.

2. The Persian word *afsus* today means "regret," but there is an older sense meaning "mockery."
   Mogh-bache (Magian child). See "Paean of a Dreg-Drinker: Notes," page 74.

4. In the Persian, *shirin-pesarân* (sweet boys) is most commonly used in manuscripts, though *shirin-dahanân* (sweet mouths) also exists.

Clarke

1. The "wet skirt" and the "stained prayer-mat" signify the sins of Hafez.

2. The magian boy is mentioned for the sake of the inculcation of spiritual truths. The sanctuary of celestial love must be approached with purity.

3. The second line may be:
   So that by thee, this cloister become not stained (*kharâb âludeh*).

4. In old age, the deeds of youthfulness do not.

6. The water (or the lustrous, water-like, honour) of the world may bestain us; not so the water of love's ocean.

7. "Water earth bestained" signifies:
   the human body (clay and water) unregenerated by God's grace.

Dŭ-ş̆ə/rāf-tām//bĕ dă/-r-ē mēy//-kă-de/xā̆-b ā̆//-lŭ̄/-dē

Dûşə, ráftam be-dár-ē meykade, xâb-âlûde;
xerqe tar, dâmán-o sajjâde şarâb-âlude.

Âmad, afsû̇sə-konân, moq-baçe̊-yē bắde-forûş;
goftə: "Bîdắrə şô, ey rắh-rô-e xâb-âlûde!

Şostoşûî kón-o ångah be-xarâbâtə xarâm,
tâ nȧ-gardad, ze-to, în dėyr-e xarâb, âlûde!

Be-havắ-ye láb-e şîrîn-pesarân, çȧndə konî
jôhȧr-ē rûhə, be-yâqû̇t-e mozâb, âlûde?

Be-tahârȧt-gozarân manzél-e pîri-yo mȧ-kon
xel'at-ē şeybə, ço-taşrȧ̊f-e şabâb, âlûde!

Pắk-o sâfî şô̇-o az-çậh-e tabî'at be-dȧr ậy:
ke safắî nȧ-dahad, ậb-e torâb-âlûde!"

Góftam: "Ey, jȧ̊n-e jahân! daftȧr-e gol, ėybî nîs
ke şavad, fȧsl-e bahâr, az-mėy-e nâb, âlûde!"

Âşenâyȧ̊n-e rȧh-ē eşqə, dar-în bȧhr-e amîq
qarqe gaştȧnd-o nȧ-gaştandə be-âb âlûde . . .

Goftə: "Hȧ̊fez, loqȧz-o nokte, be-yârân mȧ-forû ;!"
. . . Ậh, az-în lȯtf-e be-anvắ'-e etâb-âlûde . . . !

3. From the Qor'an (xxxiii.73): "We offered the precious consignment to the skys and earth and mountains. They refused to accept it and were frightened by it. Man carried it surely he is sinful, very foolish."

5. Some manuscripts (Qazvini/Ghani) begin the second half of the line with *sufian* (sufis), while others (Khanlari) begin with *hourian* (angels).

Clarke

1. *Doosh* (last night) signifies: the hidden world, the stage of the true Beloved.

As night is the forbidder of the comprehending of events; and, in it, the form of things is concealed—so in the hidden world, naught hath any one seen.

Meykhâne (the wine-house) signifies: the divine world, whence in the forms of travellers become full of wine of divine knowledge; and turn to this world.

Dar zadan-e Malayek (the door-beating of angels) signifies: their wishing to be qualified for the spectacle of the union of essence (*zât*) and of quality (*cefat*) which is the perfection of knowledge.

Gel-e Âdam sereshtan (the mixing of Adam's clay) signifies: the fermenting of Adam's nature.

The Hadis saith: "With my own hand, I (God) fermented for forty days the nature of Adam."

"Measure" signifies: the nature of Adam, wherein the angels measured the wine of love; and poured the readiness of his nature into vessels, thereby evoking upspringings of various kinds.

The *Aref* saith: "In the spiritual state, I beheld the hidden world."

The angels being veiled as to their own nature, regarded none superior to themselves; and became seekers of that spectacle-place of union (of essence and quality) in the hope that God would pour into their vessels of readiness the wine of love from the wine-house of the divine world.

Since the angels had not the readiness for this spectacle-place, the door of search was shut in their face.

Although the angels, by virtue of their grace and light, thought: "We are the spectacle-place of union and the possessors of this sense."

God said: "We are your God: we know that in you is no readiness. This readiness is another's who hath the capacity of grace (for good) and of grossness (for evil).

"Save one quality (grace and light), ye have naught. Ye have not the grossness of body, the bearer of the load of deposit (of love).

God kneaded Adam's clay, and, into his nature, poured a measure of the wine of divine knowledge; evoked from his nature the upspringing of divine knowledge, so that from his nature the wonders of divine mysteries issue; exalted his nature by the pure soul and the holy spirit; and arranged within him all the creation and the wonders that are in the world.

Thus, Adam acquired grace of soul with grossness of body; and became the bearer of the load of deposit of divine knowledge.

None but he hath this divine quality.

The load of the deposit of divine knowledge, God offered to those:

of the sky, who are the angels.

of the earth, who are the beasts and all animals.

of the mountains, who are the lions and the birds.

They, through want of capacity, accepted it not.

For those of the sky (the angels) have grace; but not grossness of body and the composition of darkness to do evil.

Those of the earth and the mountain have grossness of body and the composition of darkness to do evil; but not grace and light (the quality of the holy soul).

"That deposit man carried."

Adam who united grace of soul (to do good) and grossness of body (to do evil) had the readiness for that deposit; and accepted it.

Dŭ-ş^ə/dīd-am//kĕ mă/-lâ-yek//dă-r-ĕ/mēy-xân//-ĕ ză-/dānd

Dûş^ə dîdam ke malâ-yek dar-e mĕy-xâne za-dand;
gel-e âdam be-sereşt-and-o be pĕymâne za-dand.

Sâkenân-ē haram-ē setr-o afâf-ē malakût,
bâ man-ē râh neşin, bâde-ye mastâne za-dand.

Âsemân bâr-e amânat na-tavânest^ə kaşid;
qo-re-yē kâr^ə, benâm-ē man-e divâne za-dand.

Jang-e haftâd-o do mellat, hame râ ozr^ə be-neh;
çon^ə nadîd-and haqîqat, rah-e afsâne za-dand.

Şokr-e izad ke miân-ē man-o û solh oftâd.
sûfian raqs^ə-konân, sâqar-e şokrâne za-dand.

Âtaş, ân-nîst ke az şo'le-ye û xan-dad şam;
âtaş, ân-ast, ke dar xarman-e parvâne za-dand.

Kas ço Hâfez nagoşâd az rox-e andişe nĕqâb;
tâ sar-ē zôlf-e soxan râ be-qalam, şâne za-dand.

Some say this is a "poem of initiation," in the presence of the Grand Master (*Pir-e Moghân*). Corbin refers to it as the search for the Holy Grail in the mysteries of the heart of the Perfect Man. Clearly it is a poem in the tradition of the masters of enlightenment.

1. & 4. For the cup of Jamshid, see Dehkhoda and H. Corbin.

Although Ferdowsi first attributes to Kei-Khosro, an ancient Persian king, the cup with world-revealing powers, it is nonetheless known throughout Iran as *Jâm-e Jam* (cup of *Jam*—short for Jamshid). Jamshid, in ancient Persian legend, was the first man (in the *Shahnameh* of Ferdowsi he was the fourth king), the son of the sun (*Jam-Yima* and *Shid-sun*). The symbolic meanings ascribed to *Jâm-e Jam* include an astrolabe, a mirror, and a globe with the power to sometimes view and sometimes show the world; spiritually they are wisdom, the soul, and the quality of knowing oneself. In ancient times Persians etched on both cups and stones the circles of the heavens (planes of the equinox), which were also the origins of the astrolabe. With the development of astronomy, astrolabes became more and more sophisticated and were in fact the precursors of the compass, the sextant, the telescope, and also the horoscope. One face of the astrolabe would enable determination of stellar altitudes and theoretical calculations and therefore enable physical navigation. The other side gave astrological tables and the signs of the zodiac and the planets.

5. *Gonbad-e minâ mikard* literally means "enameled the dome" (of the sky).

7. The Persian word *aql* (reason) is used in some manuscripts instead of *khish* (self) in the Qazvini/Ghani text.

In the Qor'an it was Samiri who built a calf by melting the gold jewels of the Israelites and misled them to worship it. In the Bible it was Moses' brother, Aaron (Qor'an xx Ta Ha 85; Bible Exodus 32).

Clarke

7. When Musa cast down his staff, it became a serpent; when, into his arm-pit, he put his withered hand and brought it forth, the hand appeared luminous as the sun.

See Exodus vi, 1-6; vii, 10-12, and the Qor'an vii, 104-105.

As, opposed to the staff and the white hand of Musa, the sorceries of the sorcerer Samiri were ineffective, so, opposed to love (of God) and to the Pir of the Magians (the *Murshed*), the sorceries of reason are useless.

8. **Shaikh Husain Mansur Hallaj** was (919 A.D.) sentenced to death for saying: "[*Ana'l-Haqq*] I am the truth (God)."

They cut off his hands and his legs; plucked out his eyes; cut out his tongue; and beheaded him.

9. Jibra'il, Gabriel signifies. the angel of revelation, who gave to Mohammad the Qor'an; and to the Virgin Mary the promise of a Holy Son.

The word Jibra'il signifies: "the power of God."

See the Qor'an ii 91; iii, 40-42; xix, 16-19; xxi, 91; lxvii, 12.

The names of Jibra'il are: *Sarosh* (the messenger), *Ravân-bakhsh* (the soul-bestower),*Ruh-ol-Qodos* (the Holy Spirit).

Sắ-lʰ/-hắ dēl// tă-lặ/-b-ē Jặ//-m-ē Jă/-m āz mắ// mĩ / kār(d)

Sâlʰ hâ, del, talắb-e Jắm-e Jam, az-mắ mî-kard:
v-ắn-çe xởd dâştʰ, ze-bîgâne tamannắ mî-kard.

Gôhắrî k-az sadắf-ē kởn-o makân bîrûn-ast,
talab, az-gomşodegắn-ē lắb-e daryắ, mî-kard.

Moşkẻl-ē xîşʰ, bar-ē Pỉr-e Moqân, bởrdam, dûş,
k-û, be-ta'yỉd-e nazar, hẳll-e mo'ammắ mî-kard.

Dỉdam-aş, xorrắm-o xandân, qadẳh-ē bâde be-dast;
v-andar ân âyene, sad gûne, tamâşắ mî-kard.

Gởftam: "în Jắm-e Jahân-bîn, be-to kẻy dâdʰ Hakîm?"
Goftʰ: "ân-rûzʰ-ke în gombẳd-e mînắ mî-kard . . ."

Bî-dẻlî, dar-hame ahvâlʰ, Xodâ bâ-'ẳ bûd;
û nẻ-mî-dỉd-aş-o, az-dûr, Xodârắ mî-kard.

În hame şo'badẻ-ye xîşʰ, ke mî-kard înjâ,
Sâmerî, pỉş-e asắ-o yad-e beyzắ, mî-kard.

Goftʰ: "ân-yârʰ, k-az-û gaştʰ sằr-ē dârʰ boland,
jởrm-aş ỉn bûdʰ ke asrắrʰ, hoveydắ mî-kard.

Fẻyz-e Rûh-ol-Qodos, ẳr, bâzʰ, madad farmâyad,
dîgarân-ham bở-konand, ân-çe Masîhắ mî-kard."

Gởftam-aş: "Selselẻ-ye zởlf-e Botân, az-pey çî̀-st?"
Goftʰ: "Hâfez, gelẻ̂î az-dẻl-e şeydắ mî-kard . . ."

7. The caravan and the fire are symbolic of the nomadic life (and our transient existence).

The "Ah" (breath of despair) is a sign of sincerity, and will burn the hypocrite (woollen coat) of the falsely devout.
The medical tradition of vital breath (heat) comes from Galen through Razi and Ibn Sina. A person was supposed to emit part of his soul (life) when he sighed.

Clarke

3. *Mehr-e giah* (love-grass) signifies:
   (a) a plant such that whoever hath it near him is kindly treated by all.
   (b) the mandrake.

7. In this path is no entrance for the *kherqe* (of hypocrisy).

Mǎ bě/-dĩn dār// nǎ pě/-y-ē hěṣ//-mǎ-t-ŏ-/jǎ-h ǎ//-mǎ-dě/-ĩm

Mâ, be-d-în dar, nǎ pėy-e heṣmȧt-o jȧh âmadė-îm;
az-bȧd-ē hâdese, injȧ, be-panȧh, âmadė-îm.

Rahrȯ-ē manzėl-e ėṣq-îm-o ze sar-hȧdd-e adam,
tâ, be-eqlȋm-e vojûḍ, în-hame rȧh âmadė-îm.

Sabzė-yē xȧtt-e to dȋdîm-o, ze-bostȧn-e beheṣt,
be-talabkârȧ-ye în mehrᵊ-giyȧh, âmadė-îm.

Bâ-çonîn gȧnjᵊ, ke ṣod xâzėn-e û Rȯh-e Amîn,
be-gedấî, be-dȧr-ē xânė-ye Ṣȧh, âmadė-îm.

Langȧr-ē hėlm-e to, ey kaṣtỉ-ye tôfîqᵊ, kojȧ-st?
ke, dar în bȧhr-e karam, qȧrq-e gonȧh âmadė-îm.

Ȧb-e rû mî-ravaḍ; ey, ȧbr-e xatâ-pûṣᵊ, bė-bâr!
ke, be-dîvȧn-e amal, nâme-siyȧh âmade-îm.

Hâfez, în xerqė-ye paṣmîne, bỉ-yandâzᵊ, ke mâ
az-pėy-ē qâfele, bâ-âtȧṣ-e ȧh, âmadė-îm!

Hafez's handwriting from a manuscript copy of the Khamsa of Amir Khusrau Dihlavi (dated 1355) held in the Depository of the Institute of Oriental Studies, Tashkent.

Very little factual biographical information exists on the life of Hafez. He was born in Shiraz around 1320 and died around 1390. It is said his father, a merchant who had migrated from Isphahan to Shiraz, died early. We know Hafez was well-educated, married, had at least one son, worked as a copyist, and was a poet.

The following are, however, some of the most colorful anecdotes variously told about him since his death.

Teymour, better known in the West as Timur, Tamerlane, or Tamberlane, was a Mongol heir who had conquered half the [known] world.

Although Teymour was illiterate, he surrounded himself with the learned: Persians were the historians, Arabs were prized for their algebra and geography, and Hindus for astronomy, while his spies disguised themselves as Jews.

Teymour lived in an ocean of intrigue, the bottom of which no one could see. Amirs and fakirs, priests and circus entertainers, unscrupulous wrestlers, athletes, criminals, craftsmen, the elegant and the vagabond, the arms dealer and the hermit—all worked for Teymour. He was one of the first masters of disinformation and famous for his tricks.

When Teymour invaded Shiraz in 1387 (the same year he had massacred 70,000 people in Isphahan), he apparently sent for Hafez and asked, "Is it you who has said that for a mole on the lip of a Turk you would give up my finest cities, Samarqand and Bokhara?" "Yes," replied Hafez. "What!" cried Teymour in anger. "I have captured half the world, razed cities to the ground, devastated kingdoms, and developed two magnificent cities, where I have gathered my trophies. All this is nothing to a little Persian like you! For the mole of a Turk you would give up my two finest cities?"

"My lord," replied Hafez, "it is because of generosity such as this that I stand before you today a poor beggar."

Teymour smiled and offered Hafez the robe of poet laureate.

> If that Turk of Shiraz gain our heart,
> For his dark mole, I will give Samarqand and Bokhara.

اگر آن ترک شیرازی بدست آرد دل ما را

بخال هندویش بخشم سمرقند و بخارا را

(traditional tale, retold)

Shakh-e Nabat, a woman whose name means a branch of crystal sugar, is said to have been Hafez's lover.

Hafez looked upon the prophet Khezr as one of his special guardians. About four Persian miles from Shiraz there is a place called Pir-e-Sabz, the Old Green Man; whosoever should pass forty nights in it without sleeping, on the fortieth night Khezr would appear to him and confer upon him the immortal gift of song and poetry.

Hafez in his youth fell in love with a beautiful girl of Shiraz, Shakh-e-Nabat, and to win her heart he determined to meet Khezr and receive from him the art of poetry. For thirty-nine mornings he paced beneath the windows of Shakh-e-Nabat, at noon he ate, then he slept, and at night he kept watch, undismayed by the terrible apparition of a fierce lion which was his nightly companion. At length, on the fortieth morning, Shakh-e-Nabat called him into her house and told him that she was ready to become his wife, for she preferred a man of genius to the son of a king.

Though Hafez had now gained his original end, he was now filled with desire to become a poet, and insisted upon keeping his fortieth vigil. That night an old man dressed in green garments came to him and brought him a cup of the water of immortality.

(Gertrude Bell, 1897)

Imad-e Faqih was a cleric and a poet with whom Hafez was in competition.

Shah Shuja had a great opinion of a poet named Imad-i Faqih ("the Jurisconsult") of Kirman, who is said to have taught his cat to follow him in its genuflections when he performed his prayers. This achievement was accounted by the Prince to be almost a miracle, but by Hafez to be a charlatan's trick. Accordingly, in one of his poems Hafez chided:

> *The Sufi hath made display of his virtues and begun his blandishments;*
> *He hath inaugurated his schemings with the juggling heavens.*
> *O gracefully-moving partridge who walks with so pretty an air,*
> *Be not deceived because the cat of the ascetic hath said its prayers!*

صوفی نهـاد دام و سرِحقّه بازکرد   بنیاد مکر با فلکِ حقّه باز کرد

ای کبکِ خوشِ خرام که خوش میـــــروی بناز   غرّه مشو که گربهِ زاهد نماز کرد

Shah Shuja was one of the princes during Hafez's time in Shiraz.

On one occasion the Prince [Shah Shuja] criticized Hafez's verse on the grounds of its many-sided aspects: no one motive, he complained, inspired it; it was at one moment mystical, at another erotic and bacchanalian; now serious and spiritual, and again flippant and worldly, or worse. "True," replied Hafez, "but in spite of all this everyone knows, admires and repeats my verses, while the verses of some poets whom I could name never go beyond the city gates."

Auguries are taken even today by opening Hafez's divan at random with a question in mind.

. . . when Hafez died, some of his detractors objected to his being buried in the Muslim equivalent of consecrated grounds, but that, on an augury being taken from his poems to decide the question, the following very appropriate verse resulted:

Withhold not thy footsteps from the bier of Hafiz
For, though he is immersed in sin, he will go to Paradise!

قدم دریغ مدار از جنازهٔ حافظ

که گرچه غرق گناهست میرود به بهشت

(E.G. Browne, p. 281, 280, 316, vol. III)

A F T E R W O R D

What is especially intriguing and perhaps even unique in world literature about the special place which Hafez (c. 1320-1390) has in both the Persian pantheon and the hearts of his fellow countrymen is the fact that even for today's Iranian poets, living six hundred years after his death, Hafez's five hundred or so *ghazal* poems remain ultimate models, relevant in aesthetic, cultural, and political senses.

Hafez was a kindred spirit and poetic ideal for Forugh Farrokhzad (1935-1967), Iran's most famous female literary figure in history and a leading modern poet. There are palpable echoes of Hafez in Farrokhzad's poetry, and she once opined, "O, I wish I could compose poetry like Hafez and like him possess the sensitivity to establish a relationship with all of the intimate moments in the lives of all future humankind."[1] On another occasion, Farrokhzad went so far as to assert provocatively that Hafez was perhaps the only true poet [*sha'er*] in Iran's pre-modern literary past, while most of the other so-called poets were essentially versifiers [*nazem*].[2] In this view, she echoes the words of Nima Yushij (1895-1960), the 'father' of modern Persian poetry, who acknowledges Hafez's deserved preeminence and laments the fact that Iran has always had so few *sha'ers* and so many *nazems*.[3]

The popular poet Nader Naderpur (b. 1929) consciously reflects on Hafez for inspiration in his own verse and during the 1970s even conducted private seminars in Tehran on Hafez's poetry. In self-exile since mid-1982 and residing in Los Angeles since mid-1986, Naderpur focusses much attention on Hafez in private literature classes he there conducts for Iranian émigrés.[4]

Leading contemporary poet Ahmad Shamlu (b. 1925), a steadfastly *engagé* and *opposé* voice, devoted years to editing Hafez's poems, publishing his efforts in a 1975 volume, twice reprinted since.[5] In addition, Shamlu has boldly and matter-of-factly asserted in an interview that, after decades of reading poets from various literary cultures, he had reached the conclusion that the best lyric poet in the history of world literature was Iran's own Hafez.[6] The prominent poet Mehdi Akhavan-e Sales (b. 1928) has also said as much, in

---

[1] Forugh Farrokhzad, as quoted from a letter to Ebrahim Golestan, *Javdaneh Forugh Farrokhzad* [Immortal Forugh Farrokhzad], compiled by Amir Esma'ili and Abolqasem Sedarat (Tehran: Marjan, 1968), p. 17. For a discussion of echoes of Hafez in Farrokhzad's verse, see Michael Hillmann, *A Lonely Woman: Forugh Farrokhzad and Her Poetry* (Washington, D.C.: Mage Publishers and Three Continents Press, 1987), pp. 78, 97-98, and 116-118.

[2] As reported in an interview conducted by Sadroddin Elahi, *Sepid va Siyah*, no. 801 (5 Esfand 1967); reprinted in *Immortal Forugh Farrokhzad*, pp. 110-111; discussed by Hillmann, *A Lonely Woman*, pp. 61-62. In the interview, the filmmaker and litterateur Ebrahim Golestan (b. 1922) seconds Farrokhzad's view.

[3] Nima Yushij, *Harfha-ye Hamsayeh* [Words with My Neighbor], first edition (Tehran: Donya, 1972), p. 104. Because classical Persian poetry exhibits strict adherence to conventional patterns of rhyme meter, figures of speech, and the like, modernist critics and readers often question the poetic appeal of much of it. This controversial issue is addressed in Michael Hillmann, "Manuchihri: Poet or Versifier?" *Edebiyat* (1976): 93-110.

[4] Forty Naderpur poems in translation appear in *Literature East & West* 22 (1986): 31-86. In conversation with the author in Austin, Texas in April 1984, the poet described his Hafez seminars. In a telephone conversation in February 1987 from Los Angeles, Naderpur described his classes there.

[5] Ahmad Shamlu, editor, *Hafez-e Shiraz* [Hafez of Shiraz], first edition (Tehran: Morvarid, 1975).

[6] Idem, "Harfha'i az A. Bamdad" [Comments from A. Bamdad (Ahmad Shamlu)], *Andisheh va Honar* 5, no. 2 (Spring 1965): 144.

different words.[7] As an American who loves his Shakespeare, Wordsworth, and Eliot and as a Persianist who has been reading Hafezian *ghazals* for twenty years, I cannot say I disagree with Shamlu and Akhavan.

In any case, echoing the approbation and admiration that began in the poet's own lifetime six centuries ago, Iranian writers, readers, and critics today remain almost unanimous in thinking of Hafez as the poet's poet in the Persian language and as the literary artist who best represents cultural and aesthetics ideals past and present. Specifically, they recognize him as the culminating phenomenon in the brilliant lyric verse tradition that began in Greater Khorasan with Rudaki (d. 940/1) and others some five centuries before him. Hafez's poems, accordingly, exhibit a final harmony of the separate strains of descriptive, amatory, didactic, homiletic, mystical, and panegyric expression which developed severally and then partially merged in earlier periods of Persian poetry.

Operating in a classicist tradition, Hafez owes debts to his predecessors that are obvious and substantial. Some thirty of his *ghazals* exhibit the same end rhyme scheme, metrical pattern, and subject of *ghazals* by his illustrious Shirazi predecessor Sa'di (13th c.), the acknowledged master of the courtly *ghazal* before Hafez and the stylist *par excellence* in Persian lyric poetry. However, in each instance of Sa'di's influence, Iranian critics and scholars are quick to argue that Hafez adds to his model, the result being a richer poetic statement.[8] "Morning Light" (no. 2, above) is an example of a Hafezian *ghazal* based on a Sa'di model. Another example of borrowing and enriching is "Rendezvous" (no. 8), which Hafez composed with an eye and ear to earlier *ghazals* by no fewer than eight poets, beginning with the Sufi poet Sana'i (d. 1150/1). Hafez's is clearly a culmination and the richest of the lot.[9]

The courtly tradition in Persian poetry in which Hafez is the lyric apogee exhibits a number of hallmarks, none more important than the fact that such lyric verse was almost always intended to be recited and heard rather than to be read silently. This implies the culture-specific nature of Hafez's *ghazals* as performance, to which the conventional citation of the poet's own *nom de plume*, usually in the final couplet, contributes a great deal. For any full appreciation of such Hafezian poems as the foregoing twelve *ghazals*, that they are meant to be acted out, so to speak, needs bearing in mind. In addition, readers unfamiliar with Persian need to know that all constituent lines of any given *ghazal*, as indicated in the foregoing transliterated texts, exhibit a uniform quantitative metrical pattern and a uniform end rhyme pattern of aa, ba, ca, etc., sometimes involving nearly half the syllables in a line. The pervasiveness of the rhyme schemes in "Dance of Life" (no. 4) and "Love's See" (no. 9) plays no small role in whatever appeal those two *ghazals* have for readers, in whom a pleasurable sense of anticipation-fulfillment develops as the poet maintains the monorhyme throughout the *ghazal*. Various features of the Persian language, including flexible word

[7] Mehdi Akhavan-e Sales, *Arghenun* [The Organ], second printing (Tehran: Morvarid, 1969, p. 168).
[8] E.g., 'Ali Dashti, "Zaban-e Sa'di" [Sa'di's Language], *Naqshi az Hafez* [A Portrait of Hafez], fifth printing, revised (Tehran: Amir Kabir, 1970), pp. 216-248.
[9] Ibid., pp. 37-55.

order, make it possible for such verse to seem very natural despite what might appear to outsiders as restrictive poetic conventions. All of the technical conventions of the medieval Persian *ghazal* are conducive to the appeal of poetry as recited. Thus, when Hafez indulges in self-praise at the end of a *ghazal*, as in the case of "The Veil" (no. 10), he draws attention to the text as poetry being performed, in which no attempt is made to hide artifice and in which, often as not, the single personality of the performer-speaker establishes the unity or integrity of the performance.

Echoes of Omar Khayyam (1048-1131) likewise abound in Hafez's *ghazals*, as readers familiar with Edward FitzGerald's relatively accurate reflection of Khayyamic themes and tone in *The Rubaíyát of Omar Khayyám* (4th edition, 1879) will no doubt have recognized. From Khayyam, Hafez received poetic encouragement to voice and prize the value of the moment and to dare to question received values. These two themes are clearly embodied in the *ghazal* entitled "Song of Spring" (no. 1). In the more famous *ghazal* called "Paean of a Dreg-Drinker" (no. 5), Khayyamic influence appears in the assertion of the fruitlessness of rational inquiry, the observation of the cruelty of fate, the recognition of the transience of things, and taking solace in forbidden wine. Altogether, the poem voices a daring, almost blasphemous Khayyamic disregard for the values of the political and religious establishment of the poet's day.

In that poem, Hafez's stance can best be summarized in a single word in the next-to-last line, where the speaker advises himself to drink wine, behave as a *rend*, and be happy. "Profligate," "libertine," "reckless freespirit," and "uninhibited lover" are English equivalents which scholars and translators have employed to communicate the sense of the Persian term.[10] Hafez's continuing popularity, especially among secular intellectuals, has much to do with the perception of him as a *rend*, this ardent individualist and nonconformist who is unconcerned with or unconstrained by prevailing mores, this lover of life and love who wholeheartedly holds his exterior up for reproach (either because of a lack of concern for what people may think or because of a deliberate courting of disfavor), while possessing a privately moral character. The special appeal of Hafez's *rend* personality—and the word *reṇḍ* appears scores of times in his poetry—is manifold. First is the significance of behaving without regard to one's reputation in a culture in which propriety, formality, and approved style counted for so much. In other words, persons who cannot afford to be reckless in their own behavior often prize such qualities in the vicarious experiences of mythologized historical figures in their own culture. Second, insofar as those political concerns and fears endemic in absolute monarchical environments have always been a major reason for circumspectness in Iran, behavior that exhibits disregard for public opinion strikes many privately dissident individuals as heroically anti-establishment. Hafez's poetic personae have con-

[10] A recent definition of *rend* is provided by Julie Scott Meisami, "The World's Pleasance: Hafez's Allegorical Gardens," *Comparative Criticism* 5 (1983): 172 and 184, note 51: "a drinker of wine, poet, lover, and something of a philosopher as well–who embodies the virtues of independence, honesty, compassion, and total dedication to love, and who has reached the state of contentment denied to the ascetic and his ilk because of their preoccupation with the affairs of this world. The *rend* . . . celebrates life with wine." She adds that: "the *rends* were 'brotherhoods' which practised the virtues connected with chivalry and courtesy and opposed themselves, through their assumption of the guise of libertinism, to the interests of the religious hierarchy."

vinced many Iranians that he courageously resisted the political orthodoxy of his day, which he most assuredly could not have afforded to do as a prominent court poet.[11] Third is the sheer romantic appeal of individualistic behavior for those who cannot achieve great public individuality in a patriarchal culture in which the only true individuals have generally been the monarch or religious leader or their representatives.

Besides the presumed individualism and stoicism of a philosophical Khayyam and the masterful craft and wit of a Sa'di, readers have long also sensed in Hafez's poetry a special intensity of feeling, sincerity, and depth of experience, qualities that bring immediately to mind the poetry of Jalaloddin Rumi (1207-1273), the premier Sufi poet in history and another chief influence on Hafez.

Sufism or Islamic mysticism includes that approach to the Moslem faith and its practice in which Moslems seek to find the truth of divine love and knowledge through the personal experience of God rather than through conventional and institutionalized religious practices and rituals. Some scholars believe that the very devastation of the Mongol invasions stimulated Sufism in the thirteenth century as a consolation for the hardships of this world. Sufism had existed by this time for hundreds of years, having grown out of reactions to the worldliness of the Omayyad Caliphate (661-749) on the part of devout ascetics who emphasized the Koran's stern warnings about Judgment Day. Piety and the forsaking of worldly things were hallmarks of these early Sufis. Their name presumably derives from the Arabic word *suf* [wool] in reference to coarse woollen garments some of them wore to demonstrate their rejection of creature comforts. Then there developed a mysticism of love in which the Sufi endeavors out of love for God to lose him-or herself in love and God.

Sufism was a phenomenon that inspired and drew inspiration from every corner of the Islamic world. But its most brilliant exposition in art was in Persian poetry. As a major mode of poetic expression from Abu Sa'id Ebn-e Abi-l-Khayr (d. 1048) to Jami (1414-1492), Sufism represented specific attitudes and answers to life's dilemmas and travails. It is at one extreme of a Persian cultural spectrum of attitudes toward the material world and life in it. The Khayyamic view involves acceptance of this world in a spirit of resignation without optimism or confidence, because the future offers nothing but the interminable darkness of non-existence. A contrasting attitude is represented in Ferdowsi's much beloved, eleventh-century redaction of the Iranian national epic called *Shahnameh* [Book of Kings]. Ferdowsi depicts a world which Allah has designed and guides with his own reasons which Iranians must accept for having permitted their glorious, ancient civilization to suffer ignominious defeat at the hands of the Moslem Arabs. In his *Shahnameh*, Ferdowsi also communicates an ultimate optimism with respect to one's potential rewards in the next world, whereas in this

---

[11] As G.M. Wickens' review in "Hafiz," *Encyclopaedia of Islam: New Edition* 3 (1971): 55-57, demonstrates, no more is known about Hafez's life than about the lives of such famous predecessors as Ferdowsi and Khayyam. In fact, to observe that Hafez was born in Shiraz around the year 1320, received a sound education, worked for a time as a scribe, was a professional poet formally associated with several successive rulers' courts there, travelled little, had an intimate knowledge of the Koran and Persian literature, composed some five hundred *ghazal* poems and a handful of poems in other verse forms, was famous in his own lifetime, and died around 1390, practically exhausts the indisputable biographical facts. In the first important bio-bibliographical sketch of Hafez in English, E.G. Browne, "Hafiz of Shiraz," *A Literary History of Persia*, volume 3 (Cambridge: Cambridge University Press, 1969 [first published in 1920]), pp. 271-319, presents most of the unsubstantiated lore recorded in Persian chronicles.

world even all-powerful monarchs and the matchless warrior-hero Rostam die, and before him his son Sohrab.

As for Sufism in Persian literature, it begins in the same religious faith that permeates the *Shahnameh* and proceeds to a rejection of the inherent worth of this world, seeing it merely as an unworthy reflection of another. Much Sufi activity was orthodox. But, like individualistic Khayyamic resignation, that segment of the Sufi movement which advocated an individualistic search for God and rejection of institutional intermediaries posed a threat to governmental and religious establishments. A classic example is Mansur al-Hallaj (d. 922), the Sufi martyr of Baghdad to whom Hafez alludes in the phrase "that friend" in his famous *ghazal* called "Back to the Heart" (no. 11). Recognizing that his success on this mystical quest meant that what was essential in him was that which the creator put into his being, Hallaj scandalized the orthodox Moslem community by declaring *"Ana'l-haqq"* [I am the creative truth, i.e., Allah]. In addition, a consequence of Hallaj's declaration, if unchecked, was that other Moslems might be encouraged to pursue God as individualistically as he did, and thus precipitate a dramatic decrease in the power of the theocratic establishment and their control over the people at large. Therefore, the Caliphal authorities had Hallaj tortured and beheaded. In various guises and for very understandable reasons, qualities of Sufistic individualism, rejection of the blandishments of this world, and unswerving principles were and remain part of Iranian cultural life at least as *desiderata* or wishful thinking.

The facts of everyday Iranian life may have caused individualistic Sufism to be dead in today's Iran as a viable or relevant life style. As for more orthodox Sufi behavior, Hafez himself often criticizes those ascetics and Sufis who seemed to be voicing no more than hypocritical lipservice to ideals in his day. Such criticism, often in a satirical mode, is another endearing aspect of Hafez. In "Boatpeople" (no. 6), "Leave the Rest Behind" (no. 7), and "From Behind the Caravan" (no. 12), the theme is expressed in the poems' final images of the *kherqeh* [woollen cloak]. This cloak announces one as a Sufi, but under it, Hafez realizes, much can be hidden. Therefore, he recommends that it be cast aside, that one not judge or be judged by appearances. Despite this ambiguity with respect to the label "Sufi" and despite the fact that Sufism does not seem a viable banner around which to gather today, the respect many educated Iranians have for such great Sufis as Faridoddin 'Attar (d.c. 1220) and the more celebrated Jalaloddin Rumi, simply called *mowlana* [our master] in Persian, imply that Sufi values are highly prized in the contemporary world where the life of the spirit seems all too often subordinated to the life of acquisition and where ideals of equality and brotherhood are often obscured in political and social hierarchies.

Rumi's poems are powerful, often apparently spontaneous outbursts and declarations of the nobility of a soaring human spirit from the depths of his heart. They touched Hafez, and he learned from them, as he did from Sa'di's craft and Khayyam's skepticism. In such Hafezian *ghazals* as "Thorns and Roses" (no. 3), the reader senses the sort of sincerity of feeling and belief that imbue Rumi's poetry. In a poem such as "The Veil" (no. 10), Hafez depicts the seriousness of human responsibility in the scheme of things, much as Rumi did before him. In many *ghazals*, Hafez depicts love in terms that reveal a level of mystical awareness or experience. "Back to the Heart" (no. 11) is an example.

But there is more to Hafez's unique appeal than his artful incorporation of elements of Rumi's spirit into his own poetry or, for that matter, than the fact that he combines and integrates the distinctive qualities of all three of his most influential predecessors. Readers have always felt that Hafez's voice is itself distinctive, that whatever he inherited from the past became part of a special Hafezian personality that is more than a culmination of what developed before him in Persian poetry.

The prominent expatriate writer Bozorg 'Alavi (b. 1904) recalls reading Hafez regularly in prison after being incarcerated in 1937 by the Pahlavi authorities for alleged Communist activities. 'Alavi's biographer reports that on his first visit to 'Alavi's home in East Berlin in 1973, the writer insisted on reading some Hafez aloud as entertainment.[12] Such an attraction to Hafez implies a relevance more than that toward a romantic, medieval, and mythologized individualist and an interest in the poet more than that of the dilettante or academic. After all, 'Alavi has spent the bulk of his life as a politically active and dissident writer who has lived in East Germany since 1952 because he faced imprisonment or perhaps death had he dared to return to Iran while Mohammad Reza Pahlavi (ruled 1941-1979) was on the throne. At the other extreme, but equally illustrative of how seriously Hafez is taken today, is the initially unlikely interest on the part of Ruhollah Khomayni (b. 1902) in the poet. In the 1930s, Khomayni became acquainted with Hafez's *Divan* and thought of it as a model in his own attempts at composing verse. Khomayni has been observed on occasion to have been moved almost to tears at hearing Hafez's poems recited. In 1979, under the *nom de plume* "Hendi," Iran's leading Shi'i Moslem cleric published a collection of verse exhibiting obvious Hafezian influence.[13]

For the preeminent social critic of the 1960s, Jalal Al-e Ahmad (1923-1969),—and this may be a key to the poet's continuing unique appeal—Hafez is special because he epitomized "the Iranian world view." Reminding readers that "we do not seek these auguries from Hafez for nothing," Al-e Ahmad sees Hafez's quintessential Iranianness in his expression of pairs of opposites or contraries: protest and submission, ingenuousness and cleverness, faith and apostasy, endeavor and nonchalance, determinism and free will. Al-e Ahmad is implying that in Iranian culture dipolarities and dualities are part and parcel of the lives of thinking individuals and that, more importantly, cultural dilemmas are not supposed to be resolved, but rather are supposed to continue in tandem and tense harmony or harmonious conflict as cultural forces.[14] In this light, Khayyam with his skepticism, Sa'di with his cynicism, and Rumi with his reduction of "the two worlds" to one apparently cannot be wholly

[12] Donné Raffat, *The Prison Papers of Bozorg Alavi: A Literary Odyssey* (Syracuse: Syracuse University Press, 1985), pp. 42 and 52.

[13] Amir Taheri, *The Spirit of Allah: Khomeini and the Islamic Revolution* (Bethesda, Adler & Adler, 1986), pp. 59-61, 94, and 244, details Khomayni's almost lifelong interest in Hafez's poetry. As Mortaza Motahheri, *Tamashagar-e Raz: Mabahesi piramun-e Shenakht-e Vaqe'i-ye Khajeh Hafez* [Witness to Secrets: A Discussion on the Subject of True Understanding of Khajeh Hafez] (Tehran: Sadra, 1980), reveals, Shi'i clerical appreciation of the poet depends upon an interpretation of Hafez (which the *ghazal* texts do not support) as an orthodox Sufi.

[14] Jalal Al-e Ahmad, "Hafez," *Farhang-e Jalal Al-e Ahmad* [A Jalal Al-e Ahmad Dictionary], second printing, compiled by Mostafa Zamani Niya (Tehran: Pasargad, 1984/85), p. 374; and idem, *Dar Khedmat va Khiyanat-e Rowshanfekran* [On the Good Offices and Treasonable Activities of Intellectuals] (Tehran: Ravaq, 1977), pp. 176-177. Iranian cultural dualism as manifested in Persian literature is a major focus in Michael Hillmann, *Iranian Culture: A Persianist View* (Lanham, Maryland: University Press of America, 1987). Non-Persianist analyses of Iranian culture often exhibit similar views. For example, according to the historian Roy Mottahedeh, *The*

satisfying in artistic, cultural, or intellectual terms to such contemporary Iranians as Nima Yushij, Jalal Al-e Ahmad, and Ahmad Shamlu who recognize their culture's special nature. But Hafez can and is. As the social reformer and political activist 'Ali Sharia'ti (1933-1977) has put it, Hafez is the only Persian poet with whom one can develop a close friendship![15]

The honest and realistic dipolarity of the content of Hafezian *ghazals*, as in the speaker's expression of religious faith in "Thorns and Roses" (no. 3) vis-à-vis the apparent heterodoxy voiced in "Song of Spring" (no. 1), or the speaker's decision in "Rendezvous" (no. 8) to drink life's wine, whether it is the familiar intoxicant or a celestial inspirant, is only part of their dramatically engaging dualism. Hafez's appeal derives equally from the implication of such dipolarity in various verbal and rhetorical patterns of his *ghazals* and other verse components which themselves are conducive to or reflective of dualism, parallelism, balance, contrast, tension, dichotomy and the like. They run the gamut from almost ubiquitous puns to multifaceted allegory. The most obvious example of the latter appears in recurrent garden imagery, which evokes a simultaneous sense of perfect springtime gardens, idealized settings for courtly lovers, and paradise.[16]

The most discussed of such dipolar or dualistic phenomena is the rhetorical figure called *iham* [ambivalence], which some scholars consider the most distinctive feature of the Hafezian *ghazal*.[17] "Rendezvous" (no. 8) and "Back to the Heart" (no. 11) serve particularly well to illustrate dimensions of *iham*.

The opening couplets of "Rendezvous" present the reader with a very tangible and concrete picture of the ideal beloved. In the fifth couplet, the words "ascetic," "gift," and "day of creation" combine with "infidel" in the fourth couplet and the vigil scene in the third to create the sense that the love emotion is religious or that love is a religion. In the sixth couplet, the word "He" refers to God, the creator; and wine, because God created it, is accepted for whatever it is. Then, in the final couplet, the word "repentance" appears as Hafez announces that wine and the beauty of the beloved overwhelm the resolution to repent.

The net effect of such religious imagery is to convince the reader of the *ghazal's* special seriousness and to heighten the sense of the dedication and perseverance, as in a religious commitment, that the lover must be possessed of. But the imagery may do more, because there is something in the impact of the poem that defies a straightforward thematic paraphrase. The image of the beloved seems to relate only to secular love, yet . . . The warning to ascetics may relate merely to the question of judging others by appearances, yet . . . Love and wine are treated as one in terms of their worship and effects: their primary

Mantle of the Prophet (New York: Simon and Schuster, 1985), p. 164 (italics added): Medieval "Persian poetry came to be the emotional home in which the *ambiguity* that was *at the heart of Iranian culture* lived most freely and openly." Taheri, *The Spirit of Allah*, p. 59, observes that "some Iranian thinkers" see Moslem Iranian culture as the backdrop to "our national multiple schizophrenia." Al-e Ahmad, *Sangi bar Guri* [A Stone on a Grave] (Tehran: Ravaq, 1981), pp. 70ff, senses in his own cultural personality the contradictory tugs at his conscience and psyche by the modern intellectual and the traditional "eastern" man in him.
[15] 'Ali Shari'ati, *Majmu'eh-ye Asar* [Collected Works] volume 33 (Tehran: Agah, 1983), pp. 907-908.
[16] Julie Scott Meisami, "Allegorical Techniques in the *Ghazals* of Hafez," *Edebiyat* 4 (1979): 1-40; and idem, "The World's Pleasance: Hafiz's Allegorical Gardens," *Comparative Criticism* 5 (1983): 153-185.
[17] E.g., Manuchehr Mortazavi, "Iham ya Khasiseh-ye Asli-ye Sabk-e Hafez" [Ambivalence or the Essential Characteristic of Hafez's Style], *Nashriyeh-ye Daneshkadeh-ye Adabiyat-e Tabriz* 11 (1960/61): 193-224 and 485-500.

effect is loss of self, a lover is "mad," i.e., has lost self. Perhaps "love" need not be taken allegorically in "Rendezvous," because love naturally operates on several levels. But wine has no such extension of self. It is treated here, possibly wine of heaven, as if it were part of allegorical meaning. As to what it can symbolize, if "goblet" can metaphorically represent "heart," then wine is what the heart contains, the intoxicating, warm, flowing juice of loss of self, of giving, of being part of ultimate reality. The point need not be pressed. The ambivalence, however, is decidedly there. And the fact that Hafez started with Sana'i's Sufi model and proceeded to add the non-gnostic possibilities is a clear indication of an intention of creating ambivalence.[18]

The embodiment of ambivalence forces readers to think simultaneously of physical, metaphysical, and gnostic aspects of the beloved and this-worldly and other-worldly dimensions of levels of love experiences and emotions. In this regard, Hafez's is a culminating poetic imagination in a lyric tradition in which the subjects of address initially were *ma'shuq* [the beloved], *ma'bud* [the worshipped], and *mamduh* [the praised], i.e., respectively, a romantic beloved, Allah, and a royal figure or other patron. By Hafez's day, epithets, imagery, and states originally associated with only one of these three objects of poetic address had merged in multilayered, ambivalent contexts. Hafez is the master at maintaining the tension, mystery, and significance of the merging of *ma'shuq* and *ma'bud* figures, and sometimes *ma'shuq* and *mamduh*.

Hafez's very famous "Back to the Heart" *ghazal* (no. 11) serves as a perfect example of this tendency. Actually, this *ghazal* seems at the other end of the spectrum in comparison with "Paean of a Dreg-Drinker" (no. 5) because its theme operates primarily, if not exclusively, on a metaphysical, perhaps gnostic level.

The *ghazal* focusses specifically on the "cup of Jamshid" [*jâm-e jam*], an image with a history in Persian poetry back to the Ghaznavid period. For example, the following quatrain, probably composed by Ruzbehan Baqli of Shiraz (1128-1209), embodied a conventional meaning for the image:

> *In search of Jamshid's cup I crossed the world,*
> *I never rested days nor slept at night.*
> *I heard the secret from a master, so*
> *I knew the world-revealing cup was I.*[19]

---

[18] Sana'i, as quoted in Dashti, *A Portrait of Hafez*, pp. 38-39.

[19] As quoted in Parviz Natel Khanlari, compiler and editor, *Divan-e Hafez* [Collected Poems of Hafez], 2 volumes, second edition (Tehran: Kharazmi, 1983) 2: 1171. The cup of Jamshid and the world-seeing cup in the hand of the Magian elder, as in "Back to the Heart" (no. 11), are one and the same in medieval Persian literature. The meaning ascribed to them by Mahmud Shabestari (d.c. 1320) is the sense, according to Mohammad Mo'in, *An Intermediate Persian Dictionary*, intended by Hafez. Shabestari, *Kanz al-Haqa'eq* [Treasure of Truths], edited by Mohammad 'Ali Safir (Tehran: Ofset, 1965), pp. 120-122, declares that *jâm-e jam* is a symbol for "the knowing (wise) soul (self, person)" and asserts that "when man perfects his *nafs* [soul, self, person], he becomes inclusive of all creation; . . . when he becomes *'aref* [gnostic, knowing, mystic], he is the *jâm-e jam*." The cup of Jamshid, therefore, is a quality of knowing oneself and of merging with the rest of creation or with the creator. As the famous Sufi tradition goes: "He who knows his soul (self, person), knows his lord." This explains the Magian elder's assertion in "Back to the Heart" that he received the cup at the beginning of the world: it is a capacity all human beings are given from the beginning of time. It explains, as well, the allusions in the *ghazal's* sixth and seventh couplets.

In "Back to the Heart," the cup or goblet of Jamshid is described as something the speaker's "heart" has sought from him, something which the "heart" itself had, a jewel (the Persian word also denotes "essence" and "pearl") beyond time and place, which the "heart" sought from the lost ones at the edge of the sea, something the whereabouts of which the speaker hopes and expects the Magian elder to apprise him. The speaker's problem from the beginning is not so much knowing what the "cup of Jamshid" is, because he intimates in the second couplet that he knows metaphorically what it is by declaring that it resides in the heart. The speaker's concern is rather how one achieves awareness of possession of and the functions of the cup.

The image of the Magian elder is conventional in medieval Persian poetry. He is a leader of the Zoroastrians, a priest of the religion of dualism, of the forces of light and darkness, of presumed fire-worship, and monastic retreats far from cities and mundane concerns. His is a religion in which wine, intoxicating and inspiring, is not unlawful. (In practical terms, of course, Zoroastrians, Jews, and Christians could produce and sell wine, as practicing Moslems could not). So, as a figure of otherworldly mystery performing rites and worship strange to the Moslem, the Magian elder symbolizes the world of experience and esoteric knowledge. His actions in the *ghazal* reveal that he is surely a qualified guide and source of inspiration for the speaker, and it is in his words that the answer to the speaker's quest is found.

The speaker asks him: What are the chain-like tresses of the beloveds for? The Magian responds that the speaker Hafez is asking this latter question, is complaining so to speak, because of a heart in the frenzy of love, captured by the chains of the irresistible tresses of beloveds perfect enough to worship—only a lover would see those tresses as chains. By virtue of the frenzy of his heart, because of which he has relinquished his freedom and has become a captive of the beloved, Hafez has lost his self, his self-interest, his personality as distinct from the beloved's, and is actively possessed of the cup of Jamshid.

What Hafez does so masterfully in poems such as "Back to the Heart" is of continuing relevance. Because even with the emphasis in the poem on abstract concepts and metaphysicality and the concomitant and shaping ambivalence, he does not deny the secular, romantic level of love. In Rumi, the imagery used for the beloved is merely a device for representing God. In Sa'di, the perfect beloved may seem no more than the ideal courtly love mode. In Hafez, no possibilities are denied, and no faith system or philosophy imposed upon the reader who experiences in the realm of his medieval, classicist art the very dipolarity confronted at every turn in Iranian life. The poles for Iranian intellectuals may be different from those embodied in Hafezian *ghazals*. For example, Akhavan-e Sales finds himself torn between an ancient and medieval past and their cultural baggage and then to the modern present with issues of East and West, religious and secular values, materialistic demands in conflict with a need for spiritual moorings,[20] and a host of other tensions natural

[20] Sorour S. Soroudi, "The Iranian Heritage in the Eyes of the Contemporary Poet Mehdi Akhavan-Sales," *Towards a Modern Iran: Studies in Thought, Politics, and Society*, edited by Elie Kedourie and Sylvia G. Haim (London: Frank Cass, 1980), pp. 132-154, discusses the poet's intellectual dilemmas. Hillmann, *Iranian Culture: A Persianist View*, pp. 21-25, presents a translation and cultural analysis of Akhavan's famous poem called "The Ending of the *Shahnameh*" (1957), his best known reflection on the Iranian past versus the present.

to a crossroads culture with a lengthy, continuous cultural history. But today's readers find in Hafez a kindred spirit, an Iranian artist who realized as they do that there are no answers in a full and honest Iranian life, but rather that such a life, which one should live to the fullest, will always involve adjusting to the motion of a pendulum whose poles are vital to that culture's survival and health.

It is especially fortuitous that Michael Boylan's translations and Hossein Zenderoudi's illustrations appear above in tandem, creating their own ambivalence. In the main, Boylan communicates earthbound and romantic elements of Hafez's verse. The very titles he chooses for the *ghazals* in translation (which are untitled in the original Persian) and the representation of the beloveds as females (more often than not, they are males in the original Persian)[21] emphasize this interpretation. In addition, Boylan routinely chooses not to translate the metaphysical or Sufistic side to ambivalent terms and images. Nevertheless, the ease with which Hafez's mundane side comes across in English is testimony to the poet's continued relevance on that level.

On the other hand, Zenderoudi's illustrations of the poems' very words, colored masterfully, patterned, highlighted, encased, and symmetrically arranged, offer a metaphor for classicist elements in the *ghazals* and emphasize their metaphysical, otherworldly, and Sufistic aspects. For example, his illustration for "Morning Light" (no. 2) spiritualizes a courtly love poem through the repetitive clusters of the written word Allah, together with the superimposed, upward moving triangles on the vertical axis reminiscent of Zenderoudi's Sufistic painting called "Keramat" (1983).[22]

The media employed by Boylan and Zenderoudi allowed one emphasis or another. Vis-à-vis the original *ghazals*, that itself is testimony to Hafez's greatness. For he is able to bring to life both worlds, both wines, both everythings in one medium, in one *ghazal*, in one couplet or line, sometimes in a single image, or a single word.

Michael Craig Hillmann
Austin, Texas
July 1987

[21] Ehsan Yarshater, "Persian Poetry in the Timurid and Safavid Periods," *The Cambridge History of Iran*, volume 6 (Cambridge: Cambridge University Press, 1986), pp. 973-974.
[22] Hossein Zenderoudi, "Keramat," *Contemporary Persian Art: Expression of Our Time*. Pacific Asian Museum, Pasadena, California (Foundation for Iranian Studies, Washington, D.C., 1984), p. 25.

BIBLIOGRAPHY

Persian

Dashti, 'Ali. *Kakh-e Ebda'* [The Palace of Creativity]. Tehran: Majalleh-ye Yaghma, 1973.
———— . *Naqshi az Hafez* [A Portrait of Hafez]. Revised edition, fifth printing. Tehran: Amir Kabir, 1970.

Ghani, Qasem. *Tarikh-e 'Asr-e Hafez* [History of the Age of Hafez]. Tehran: Zavvar, 1943.

Goethe, Johann Wolfgang. *Divan-e Sharqi* [Der West-östlicher Divan]. Translated by Shoja'oddin Shafa. Second printing. Tehran: Ebn-e Sina, 1964/65.

Hafez. *Divan-e Hafez, Khajeh Shamsoddin Mohammad* [Collected Poems of Hafez, Khajeh Shamsoddin Mohammad]. *Volume 1: Ghazaliyat* [Ghazals]. Second printing with revisions. Edited by Parviz Natel Khanlari. Tehran: Kharazmi, 1983/84.
———— . *Divan-e Khajeh Shamsoddin Mohammad Hafez-e Shirazi* [Collected Poems of Khajeh Shamsoddin Mohammad Hafez of Shiraz]. Edited by Mohammad Qazvini and Qasem Ghani. Tehran: Zavvar, n.d., first published in 1941.

Hillmann, Michael. "Naqd-e Adabi va Divan-e Hafez" [Literary Criticism and Hafez's Divan]. *Rahnema-ye Ketab* 13 (1970): 43-52.

Mescoub, Shahrokh. *Dar Kuy-e Dust* [On the Friend's Street]. Tehran: Kharazmi, 1978.

Mortazavi, Manuchehr. "Iham ya Khasiseh-ye Asli-ye Sabk-e Hafez" [Ambivalence or the Essential Characteristic of Hafez's Style]. *Nashriyeh-ye Daneshkadeh-ye Adabiyat-e Tabriz* 11 (1960/61): 193-224 and 485-500.

Rastegar, Mansur. Compiler. *Maqalati darbareh-ye Zendegi va She'r-e Hafez* [Essays on Hafez's Life and Poetry]. Shiraz: Shiraz University, 1971.

Rownaq, Mohammad 'Ali. "Gozideh-ye Ketabshenasi-ye Pazhuheshi-ye Hafez" [A Selected Scholarly Hafez Bibliography]. *Darbareh-ye Hafez* [On Hafez]. Compiled by Nasrollah Purjavadi. Tehran: Markaz-e Nashr-e Daneshgahi, 1986. Pp. 323-333. [Among its 226 items, 79 booklength studies of Hafez are cited, many authored in recent years.]

Shebli No'mani. *She'r al-'Ajam* [Persian Poetry]. Five volumes. Translated by Mohammad Taqi Fakhr Da'i Gilani. Second Printing. Tehran: Ebn-e Sina, 1960/61.

Sudi, *Sharh-e Sudi bar Hafez* [Sudi's Commentary on Hafez]. Four volumes. Translated by 'Esmat Saffarzadeh. Second printing. Tehran: Rangin, 1968/69.

Zarrinkub, 'Abdolhosayn. *Az Kucheh-ye Rendan, darbareh-ye Zendegi va Ash'ar-e Hafez* [From the Street of the Freespirited Lovers, on the Life and Poetry of Hafez]. Fourth Printing (based on the revised and expanded second edition, 1975). Tehran: Ketabha-ye Jibi, 1985.

English

Arberry, Arthur J. "The Art of Hafiz." *Aspects of Islamic Civilization*. London: George Allen & Unwin, 1964. Pp. 344-358.
———— . "Hafiz and His English Translators." *Islamic Culture* 20 (1946): 111-128 and 229-249.

_____ . *Shiraz: Persian City of Saints and Poets*. Norman: University of Oklahoma Press, 1960.

Browne, E.G. "Hafiz of Shiraz." *A Literary History of Persia*. Volume 3. Cambridge: Cambridge University Press, 1969 (first published in 1920). Pp. 271-319.

de Bruijn, J.T.P. *Of Piety and Poetry: The Interaction of Religion and Literature in the Life and Works of Hakim Sana'i of Ghazna*. Leiden: E.J. Brill, 1983.

Dashti, Ali. *In Search of Omar Khayyam* [Dami ba Khayyam (first edition)]. Translated by L.P. Elwell-Sutton. London: George Allen & Unwin, 1971.

Hafez. *The Divan*. Translated by H. Wilberforce Clarke. New York: Samuel Weiser, 1970 (originally published in 1891).

_____ . *Fifty Poems of Hafiz*. Compiled and edited by A.J. Arberry. Cambridge: Cambridge University Press, 1962, reprinted with corrections.

_____ . *Hafiz of Shiraz: Selections from His Poems*. Translated by Herman Bicknell. London: Trubner & Co., 1875.

_____ . *Poems from the Divan of Hafez*. Translated by Gertrude Lowthian Bell. London, 1897.

Hillmann, Michael C. *Iranian Culture: A Persianist View*. Lanham, Maryland: University Press of America, 1988.

_____ . *Unity in the Ghazals of Hafez*. Minneapolis: Bibliotheca Islamica, 1976. [This study includes a relatively comprehensive bibliography of materials on Hafez in European languages.]

Meisami, Julie Scott. "Allegorical Gardens in the Persian Poetic Tradition: Nezami, Rumi, Hafez." *International Journal of Middle East Studies* 17 (1985): 229-260.

Pursglove, Parvin. "Translations of Hafiz and Their Influence on English Poetry Since 1771: A Study and a Critical Biography." Ph.D. Thesis, University College of Swansea, 1983.

Schimmel, Annemarie. "Poetry and Calligraphy: Thoughts about Their Interaction in Persian Culture." *Highlights of Persian Art*. Edited by Richard Ettinghausen and Ehsan Yarshater. Boulder, Colorado: Westview Press, 1979. Pp. 177-212.

_____ . *The Triumphal Sun: A Study of the Works of Jalaloddin Rumi*. London: Fine Books, 1978 [Persian Heritage Series].

Schroeder, Eric. "Verse Translation and Hafiz." *Journal of Near Eastern Studies* 7 (1947): 209-222.

Wickens, G.M. "Hafiz." *Encyclopaedia of Islam: New Edition* 3 (1971): 55-57.

Yarshater, Ehsan. "Affinities between Persian Poetry and Music." *Studies in the Art and Literature of the Near East*. Edited by Peter Chelkowki. Salt Lake City and New York: University of Utah and New York University, 1974, Pp. 59-78.

Yohannan, John D. *Persian Poetry in England and America: A 200-Year History*. Delmar, New York: Caravan Books, 1977.

ACKNOWLEDGMENTS

Permissions were kindly given by:

Stuart Carey Welch to use the double frontispiece from a Divan of Hafez, Iran, Safavid, Tabriz, ca. 1526-27, ink, opaque watercolor and gold on paper. Courtesy of The Harvard University Art Museums (Arthur M. Sackler Museum, gift of the Welch family in memory of Philip Hofer).

The Freer Gallery of Art, Smithsonian Institution, Washington, D.C., for the use of border illustrations from the Persian manuscript (Divan) *Poems of Sultan Ahmad Djalair*, ca. 1400.

The Depository of the Institute of Oriental Studies at Tashkent for their copy of Hafez's handwriting from the *Khamsa* of Amir Khusrau Dihlavi (cat. no. 2179). We thank Dr. Glenn Lowry for so kindly supplying us with a photo he personally took in Tashkent.

Many thanks to Reza Ghanadan and Habib Bahar for their valuable assistance. We also wish to express our appreciation for the excellent comments and specific improvements suggested by Michael Hillmann and Shahrokh Mescoub.

COLOPHON

Hafez, Dance of Life has been published in this first edition of 2500 softbound and 2500 hardbound copies, including a special edition limited to 50 copies. The illuminations were printed in six colors by Arnoldo Mondadori Editore, who also printed and bound the book. The type, Palatino, Goudi Old Style and International Phonetics was set by Gerry Cervenka. A cassette recording of the poems read in English by Michael Boylan and in Persian by Parviz Bahador was also made with this book. The book was designed by Najmieh Batmanglij and edited by Mohammad Batmanglij.

Double Page Frontispiece from a
Divan of Hafez
Iran, Safavid, Tabriz, ca. 1526-27
Ink, opaque watercolor and gold on paper

Library of Congress Cataloging-in-Publication Data

Hafiz, 14th cent.
    Hafez : dance of life.

    Selected poems in English and Persian.
    Bibliography: p.
    I. Boylan, Michael.   II. Title.
PK6465.Z31B69   1987   891'.5511   87-24826

ISBN 0-934211-04-3 (cloth)
ISBN 0-934211-13-2 (paperback)
ISBN 0-934211-14-0 (limited edition)

Mage Publishers, Inc.
1032 29th Street, N.W.
Washington, D.C. 20007
(202) 342-1642

Printed in Italy